Conversations with Myself

100 Stories of Faith, Hope, and Love

Volume 2

Helen Brown

Reading Stones Publishing

Copyright © Helen Brown 2023

ISBN Softcover: 978-1-923021-12-9

   eBook: 978-1-923021-13-6

All rights reserved. No part of this book may be reproduced or transmitted in any form or by any means, electronic, or mechanical, including photocopying, recording or by any information storage and retrieval system without the permission in writing by the copyright owner.

Unless otherwise stated Scriptures quoted here are from the King James Version (Authorised version). First published in 1611. Quoted from the KJV Classic Reference Bible, copyright 1983 by the Zondervan Corporation.

Published by: Reading Stones Publishing
Helen Brown & Wendy Wood

Cover Design: Craft to Cover by Wendiilou

For more copies contact the author at:

Glenburnie Homestead
212 Glenburnie Road
ROB ROY NSW 2360
Mobile: 0422 577 663
Email: Readingstonespublishing@gmail.com

Conversations with Myself

100 Stories of Faith, Hope, and Love

Volume 2

Contents

A Better New Year	9
A God of Surprises	11
A Snake is a Snake	15
A strong Tower	18
A Test Taste	19
And Jesus Came Down.	21
Are We Ready?	24
Are you a Blackberry?	26
Battle Weary	28
Beauty	30
Being a Bonsai Tree	32
Being Quarantined	36
Biblical Encouragers	38
Blessings	41
Blips	43
Buying for Survival	45
Cactoblastis	47
Call to Prayer	49
Changes	51
Christmas	53
Coals or Fire	55
Common is Special	57
Confusion	59
Country Roads	61
Covered	63
Dare to be a....	65

Dividing our Country	67
Don't Let the Cat Out	70
Encouraging Others	72
Eternity is a long time	74
Fellowship	76
Following the Rules	78
From Rock to Rock	80
God's Care in Dry Times	82
God has the Reins	85
God is NOT Surprised	87
God's Calling	89
God's Quiet Voice	93
God's Teaching	95
Grounded	97
Growth in the Dark	100
He Knows My Name	102
Hell	104
Home	106
How Embarrassing	108
I'm doomed	110
I'm going away	112
It's not over yet!	114
Job	116
Kill it with Love	118
Learning God's Way	120
Is Less More	122
Life can be a Puzzle	124
Limiting God	126

Little Things	128
Living like Gideon	130
Looking Forward or Back	132
Lost	135
Making the Bed	137
Messy Tangles	139
Mother's Day	141
Moving	143
Musical Masterpiece	145
New Shoes	147
New Year Resolutions	149
Nothing New	151
Please Bless the Bush	154
Prayer	157
Prayers for Drought Breaking Rain	162
Prayers of Blessing	165
Praying Right	167
Praying with Faith	169
Queen	171
Rattled	173
Reality Check	175
Reinvention	177
Relationship	179
Shards of Light	181
Sharing	183
Sheltered	185
Shingles	187
Skill Shortage	190

Taking up the Batton	192
Tapestry	194
Tears	196
Thankfulness in Dry Times	198
The Blame Game	201
The Feast	203
The Sun	208
This too will pass	210
Turning our Eyes to Heaven	212
Waiting	215
Wanted Qualities	216
Watching Sheep	218
What does Grown Up Australia Look Like?	220
When Are We Going to God	223
While We Wait	225
Wisdom	227
Wandering in the Wilderness.	229
More Books by the Author	231

A Better New Year

It was New Year's Day, and as I read messages on social media I saw how so many people, no matter how rough their previous year was, were looking forward in hope that the new one would be better than the last.

There just seems to be an inbuilt desire for any new year to be better than the previous one. I do not ever remember seeing messages that wished friends and family a rough or tough new year.

Each year, as each year behind us has, will bring its sadnesses, and tough moments. These might be sickness; death of loved ones, or dreams being smashed by life's circumstances.

What amazes me is that God has already seen it all.

"I am Alpha and Omega, the beginning and the end, the first and the last." Revelation 22:13.

Nothing that has happened, is happening, or will happen, surprises God.

He knows exactly what we will face this year and He gracefully withholds it from us. His revelations are strictly on a 'need to know' basis and He gets it perfectly right every time. Each challenge we face is about helping us to grow closer to him, even when it feels as if we are being punished.

No matter what the year brings, we can move forward with this verse from: Zephaniah 3:17 "Yahweh, your God, is among you, a mighty one who will save. He will rejoice over you with joy. He will calm you in his love. He will rejoice over you with singing.

As you move forward, don't forget to hold God's hand, and allow Him to help you develop another set of skills during the new year.

Prayer: Lord, help us to remember that you know exactly what we will face this year and thank you for holding us together during the tough times as well as the good ones.

A God of Surprises

Does what God does still surprise you?

All my life I wanted to write a book like Anne or Jo, my heroines in my favourite books, Anne of Green Gables, and Little Women. With my learning difficulties at school, I'm sure that my teachers would have just laughed out loud in the staff room if they had even suspected I had such a dream. Yet, in my late fifties I was able to achieve such an undertaking. I published my first book, and I was convinced then that it would be my only one.

Surprise Number 1

God found ways to keep me writing and I now have ten books, and still counting, of my own and one that I have made a significant contribution to.

With the drought giving so many of our people so much grief, with the death of animals, crops and family members who find that they can no longer cope and the extra workload of having to help my husband feed sheep on a daily basis, publishing my sixth book seemed to be out of reach. The first five, were easy, as all I did was send the material off to the publisher and they did all the hard work, such as cover design, book layout, and uploads but that service, as always, came with a price in dollars. I didn't have those dollars to spend this time. So, God arranged for many people to encourage me to do it myself. To be a true 'Self-publisher'.

"For My thoughts *are* not your thoughts, Nor *are* your ways My ways," says the LORD. For *as* the heavens are higher than the earth, So are My ways higher than your ways, And My thoughts than your thoughts." Isaiah 55:8-9.

Surprise Number 2

My daughter decided to give me a hand and so we started a very steep learning curve. Well, she certainly did. Hurdles presented themselves with annoying regularity. Firstly, my internet service kept dropping out and I wondered if I was supposed to be doing this. However, each day when we started working on the book the internet would work just until we had finished everything that we needed to do. We often finished just as my husband came home and required my services out in the paddock. Assistance with the cover was given for free and the list goes on and on. My book was a reality.

"Trust in the LORD with all thine heart; and lean not unto thine own understanding. In all thy ways acknowledge him, and he shall direct thy paths." Proverbs 3:5-6

Surprise Number 3

During this process my sister sent me some of her writings to read. I was so surprised that I didn't have a clue that my sister was so talented. However, I also knew that she wasn't keen on publishing due to a very bad experience many years ago. Eventually, she relented and allowed me to publish the story for her. God again worked in so many small ways to make it happen in order for it to be released on the 4th September, when we celebrate the memory of our mother's arrival in Heaven. This is a special day for us, and we had planned to spend each five-year anniversary together despite the thousands of miles that separate us. Due to the drought here and her pastoral work, that hasn't been possible very often.

"A man's heart plans his way, But the LORD directs his steps." Proverbs 16:9.

And they keep coming!

We found out that we could publish a second book written by my sister and I asked God to show me if it was right to do so, by giving me a particular cloud formation. I wanted it for the cover.

God had surprised me a lot back then, He moved many people and circumstances in so many different ways to bring us to the place we are. To me it was a clear indication that we were to move forward. However, no clouds appeared in the sky. Then one night while talking to my daughter, she pulled up a photo with the required cloud formation. To me God was saying, "Yes, go ahead." My daughter didn't know that I had asked for the go ahead in such a specific manner. The fact that the cloud was a photo on the internet instead of the sky just indicated to me that God's ways are different to mine.

As I look forward, I know that there will be years ahead when there will be no income from our farm. Even when it rains, it will take years for our stock numbers to increase, the native grasses will also take time to grow and we will have to find money to replant our pastures. Yet, I'm glad that God keeps reminding me that He doesn't always work inside my human mind set. He has the whole universe to work with and He will.

"Whatsoever the LORD pleased, *that* did he in heaven, and in earth, in the seas, and all deep places." Psalm 135:6.

Has God surprised you lately?

A Snake is a Snake

A young lady was moving into a new home, and summer was on its way. The previous occupants had left some piles of rubbish lying around. Knowing that these would be the favourite hiding places for snakes she requested that they be cleaned up, however, these requests to the owners were met with scepticism about the necessity of having to clean it up. There had only been a couple of snake sightings over the last ten years.

Eventually, two men turned up to take away the rubbish. All went well until the final sheet of tin was lifted, only to reveal, not one but three small snakes.

In a conversation with a friend, the young lady declared that she felt vindicated, they were only small, but they were still snakes. Now, it seems that the smaller they are the bigger the punch their poison gives.

As I thought about this later, I remembered how God considers sin. While we think there are big sins, such as murder, rape, stealing, and fraud, and small sins, which we can often have a blaze attitude towards, such like lying, cheating, anger, and gossip, but God sees them all as sins.

All sins, even the small ones, are deadly to our spiritual relationship with God. However, the best news is that unlike dealing with snakes, our relationship with God can be fixed by simply asking for His forgiveness through the death of His Son Jesus.

"For the wages of sin *is* death; but the gift of God *is* eternal life through Jesus Christ our Lord." Romans 6:23.

A Strong Tower

Being in a hurry one morning and running late for work, I didn't notice that my wallet had fallen out of my handbag as I opened the shop door. It wasn't until the Police rang me to say that it had been handed in that I even noticed that it was missing.

I collected it and the Police asked me the questions about any money that might have been in it, there were a few coins and I noticed that they were still there. However, once I got back and the relief of not having to replace all my cards wore off, I started to feel some unease about why the people who had handed it in hadn't asked me if it was my wallet when I had opened the door just after they must have retrieved it from the shop step.

I checked and my bank card was in its correct spot but then a story that I had read a few days earlier came to mind. The writer had lost all his money from his bank account without even losing his card. Somehow someone had managed to get his bankcard details online and had emptied his account. I remember thinking that I was glad that I didn't do very much online shopping and felt a little justified in not doing so.

Then I started to think about the people who had handed in my wallet. They had told the Police that they didn't look inside and therefore wouldn't have realized that I was the owner. Had they been honest with the Police or had they looked and taken my bankcard details and were planning some purchases using my account.

I felt really sad that in today's world, we automatically think the worst of people, no matter what the circumstances. I made the call to the bank, put safeguards in place, like ordering a new card, and making sure that any attempt to get money out of our account would be hard, however, by doing that it meant that until my new card arrived, the process of buying would also involve a lot more work on our behalf. The convenience of having a card was suddenly very inconvenient.

At a meeting earlier in the month, a friend had described how God had protected her husband from getting scammed with the earlier than expected arrival of their son. I found myself asking if the story about the man losing his money was God's way of making sure that we were aware of the possibility enough to take the necessary steps to protect our funds. Sure, I should have made sure that my wallet was secured in my handbag, but I could have ignored the fears, and if I was right, and money disappeared, then I would only have myself to blame. It would be unfair to blame God from not protecting our money if I hadn't done the right thing. After all, God expects us to do something, like the story of the drowning man, who rejected the people with rope, boat, and helicopter to save him from the flood waters, God gave him three opportunities to be saved and he rejected them all.

Proverbs 18:10 says: "The name of the LORD *is* a strong tower: the righteous runneth into it, and is safe." The lord is a strong tower, but we have to run into it. Like the man in the flood, God's strong tower was the rope, boat, and helicopter, in my case the bank, but we have to run into it for it to protect us.

I understand that it is not always easy to see the tower but when we do, let's not hesitate to run into it and take advantage of its protection.

A Test Taste

Do you like to taste test your cooking before you have finished the whole thing? I admit to being guilty of this.

While social distancing was law in this country, things didn't change very much for us. We were emerging slowly from the worst drought in our memory, where the number of dollars in the bank, or lack of, kept us at home more than normal anyway. While the lack of money still kept us at home, the government had added a valid excuse to not be tempted to say 'what the heck let's go somewhere anyway'. Shopping is a horrible experience.

However, I realised that for many of our country men and women this had changed their lives dramatically and drastically. I'm not going to lie, there were days when I had wanted to get in the car, visit people who were struggling, particularly my children and I shed tears aplenty after conversations over the phone with those not coping. I certainly didn't want this 'new' normal to become permanent.

As I listened to a television preacher who reminded me that this crisis is only a foretaste of what it will be like on judgement day, I felt a greater sadness for those who were not coping. I don't mean those who have a faith and are struggling with the pain that comes with having that faith stretched as we go through the new set of exercises that God has given us, but those who have no relationship with God at all.

"But he shall say, I tell you, I know you not whence ye are; depart from me, all *ye* workers of iniquity. There shall be weeping and gnashing of teeth, when ye shall see Abraham, and Isaac, and Jacob, and all the prophets, in the kingdom of God, and you *yourselves* thrust out. And they shall come from the east, and *from* the west, and from the north, and *from* the south, and shall sit down in the kingdom of God." Luke 13:27-29.

Isolation is lonely, but we have social media and telephones to keep us connected, hell will have neither of these. We wake up each morning to daylight, sunshine and a variety of colours, hell will have none of these. Even on our worst days, we know that this will someday come to an end, hell will not.

Let's go back to my original question. If you like to test taste things before you whole heartedly eat, or decide to bag it for the chooks or the bin, remember that this life is a foretaste of what is to come. It is also our only chance for all of us to decide where we are going to spend eternity. Those who do not have a relationship with God, are going to see this time as if it was a 'walk in the park'.

Those of us who are sure that this struggle is going to fade into the background against Heaven's perfection, need to pray for those for which this will only be a test taste of what is to come but will have to eat the whole horrible meal forever.

Prayer

Lord, we pray for those who have no relationship with you. We asked that your people will reach out to them so that they understand what they have to face without You.

And Jesus Came Down

2 Samuel 6:1-16.

Verse 14 "And David danced before the LORD with all *his* might; and David *was* girded with a linen ephod."

David was the King of Israel. Yet as he brings the Ark of the Covenant into Jerusalem, he makes a choice to discard his kingly attire, humble himself and dress in a plain linen ephod. Even though it would have been the best linen available, because nothing but the best was good enough to worship the Lord while they were bringing the Ark into Jerusalem, it would have felt strange and uncomfortable when compared to his normal robes of office. Yet he worships the Lord with enthusiasm and vigour.

Let's forward now to fourteen generations later. There is another King, who is trying to bring, not only the people of Israel closer to God, but the whole world.

We celebrate this event each year at Christmas time.

I noticed that there were several similarities between these two events.

Both chose to discard his kingly attire for the linen ephod. David was dressed in the same manner as a priest. He lowered himself to the level of the priests.

Jesus also chose to discard his kingly attire, the glory of Heaven, and be wrapped in swaddling cloth. Which, I suspect, were also made of linen. Jesus lowered Himself to the level of every ordinary human being.

David leads by example. He doesn't go around telling the people what to do, but he sings and dances out in front of the people, showing how it should be done.

Jesus also showed us how to live by His example. He faced every temptation that we will face and showed us that there is a right and wrong way to meet them.

David had his actions misunderstood and criticised, sure it was only by one person, his first wife, Michal. She told him that his actions were inappropriate for a man of his standing.

Jesus also faced the misinterpretations of his actions. The religious leaders of the time not only cited him for doing the will of God but the population in general expected Him to remove the bondage caused by Romans from their lives, instead of being able to remove their bondage which was a result of their sins.

David was trying to bring the children of Israel closer to God. Having the Ark back in Jerusalem would remind the people that God was their real King.

Jesus was also bringing us closer to God, not by bringing the Ark into the mist of His people but by offering Himself as a substitute for our sins.

There were also some stark differences.

Jesus went way beyond what David did. Jesus' status in Heaven was much higher than David's was on earth, David only lowered himself to the level of a priest. Jesus lowered Himself to the level of every common man. Jesus came from higher and went much lower.

While David sang and danced loudly, Jesus arrived quietly.

David offered sacrifices of animals, but Jesus offered Himself, this was a much greater sacrifice than all of those offered by David.

David was the first king of Israel to rule with a Godly heart. Jesus still reigns with a pure heart.

David died. Yes, Jesus died as well, but He is now alive, having beaten death.

David no longer reigns, yes, he has his place in Heaven but Jesus reigns there and in the hearts of all those who call Him their friend and saviour.

Are We Ready?

Are we really ready for God to bless us in our personal lives and our country?

Sitting in church, the preacher was talking about how after Jesus fed the five thousand, and how the crowd wanted to make Him king, not because they saw Him as God to be worshipped but as a magical provider of their food. The same thing occurred with the women at the well in Samaria. She initially saw Jesus' gift as a way to reduce her workload.

People are still the same, and yes, I'm guilty. As I had a conversation with a friend that afternoon, listing all the things that I knew were on my timetable for the month, I felt an overwhelming sense of being swamped, and that was without the jobs I didn't know about yet.

God started talking to me:

"I know what you have to do, don't I? I control time and I can make sure that you have enough of it to get through the things that need to be done."

"Remember, when I blessed Peter and John after they were fishing all night, (Luke 5:4-6, John 21:2-6)." Their workload really increased as they salted, sold, and did whatever they needed to do with all those fish, it wasn't a case of catch and release.

Blessings will bring more work, not less.

This is very true for our farmers, as they deal with the enormous number of weeds, storm damage, and planting that must happen, once lots of rain is received after a drought. Even mowing my backyard is a challenge. The mower had hardly been started during the two years of drought and all of sudden the grass was growing inches each day.

But I think that it's also true for our country.

The more we are blessed with children, the greater the need for scripture classes to be filled. The more people that move into an area, the greater the need for the church to reach out to them. I hear so many people today saying how they are too tired, too old, and too busy to work for Him, and yet, He knows what has to be done and He will give us the strength we need to get through it all, including resting.

"I can do all things through Christ which strengtheneth me." Philippians 4:13.

How do we tackle all those busy seasons in our lives? We stay focused on Jesus, remind ourselves regularly that He is in control and make sure that we do what we can, when we can.

Are you a Blackberry?

Blackberries, what's not to like, their fruit is delicious, and can be used to make wonderful jam, beautiful pies, and other delicious deserts.

However, particularly wild blackberry bushes grow fast, are thorny, and can make picking the fruit painful.

As I was cutting back a rather large bush, which was threating to encroach on our driveway, I noticed some interesting things that are similar to the church.

Where a cane touched the ground it grew roots, how many churches have split, only to put down roots in a different spot and start to grow diversifying God's work.

Some people like Blackberry bushes, their fruit, and what they can be made into, just like some people like Christians for their honesty, hard work, and faithfulness, but there are those who detest them, because they challenge them to think about their life choices and their eternal consequences. Like farmers, they are determined to dig out these bushes (Christians) roots and all, but I noticed that Blackberry roots run a very long way, hidden underground, and often another plant appears a long, long way from the parent plant. Christians are like those roots, we are fed by the Holy Spirit, ready to appear wherever God takes us. It's a fruitless task, trying to tame a Blackberry bush, I know I've tried, and we can be thankful that God feeds and cares for us no matter how hard those who don't appreciate the blessings of God try to dispose of us.

So, be a blackberry, fruitful, prickles and all, even if you have to run underground and pop up somewhere else, God will care for you even in the face of great trauma.

Battle Weary

"Jesus Christ is the same yesterday, today, and forever." Hebrews 13:8.

"Then the King will tell those on his right hand, 'Come, blessed of my Father, inherit the Kingdom prepared for you from the foundation of the world;" Matthew 25:34.

During a discussion about a particular problem the comment was made; "I think people are too tired to fight anymore." There have been many times when I have said much the same thing concerning my problems, particularly if they have taken a very long time to be solved.

This time, however, I thought about things a little differently. What was a long time to God? How many years did the people of Israel have to wait for God to let them into the Promised Land? How many days did Jesus stay in the Wilderness? What would happen if God ran out of patience waiting for us to answer His call? 2 Peter 3:8 tells us "But do not forget this one thing dear friends: With the Lord a day is like a thousand years, and a thousand years are like a day." And verse nine says: "The Lord is not slow in keeping his promise, as some understand slowness. He is patient with you, not wanting anyone to perish, but everyone to come to repentance."

The people of Israel wandered in the wilderness for forty years and Jesus fasted for forty days. We are so used to things being "instant" that I feel we sometimes expect God to change His ways to the "instant variety" as well. God does not change.

Life will always be a battle. It is that way because sin has entered the world. God wants us to carry on with faith in His strength, so that when we reach the end of our lives, He will be able to take great delight in welcoming us home.

Beauty

We were cleaning up my mother-in-law's house and came across, amongst a lot of other things, a whole pile of handmade doilies. As I washed them and hung them on the line, I lamented that we no longer use such beautiful things in our houses, or if we do it is limited.

I get it, they create work. They have to be washed regularly, ironed and most people, particularly working mothers, no longer have the time for such frills.

I remember my mother telling me that when my father caught her ironing sheets in the early days of their marriage, he told her that if she stopped ironing sheets, she would have more time for God's work.

Even when I was working, ironing was the one job that got out of hand very quickly. I was able to solve this problem by getting the children to do their own ironing. However, it wasn't long before most of the clothes that they wore didn't need ironing.

I, myself, have scoffed at videos showing the most amazing skills of some people with food, cakes and chocolate and I find myself thinking 'why would you bother? That's a lot of hard work for something that is only going to be eaten and never seen again'.

However, this morning I was very conscious that by making our lives, housework, and even gardens, more efficient, we have lost a very valuable thing, beauty.

It is hard work being creative, making things with lots of colour, and most people don't appreciate how much is involved, but God made beautiful things for us to enjoy and by not making the effort, I think some of us have missed out on some very valuable therapy.

All the way through history, people have built or made beautiful things to honour our God, we cannot make anything that will outshine His work, but we can use what skills he has given us to show our love for Him, and brighten up our own lives as well.

Being a Bonsai Tree

What do you think when you look at a Bonsai tree? Do you see them as ugly and distorted or a masterpiece of art? Do you admire the skills that have created such a masterpiece? Do you feel sorry that something that could have been so majestic is now confined by wire, poor soil, and a small pot? You see, the DNA of a Bonsai tree is exactly the same as its free growing specimen that stands tall in the wilderness, and yet you get two trees that look completely different in shape and size.

If you were to take two seedlings and you planted one in good rich soil with plenty of space and sunshine and the other was potted in order to create a bonsai. Their DNA and age are exactly the same. The differences are brought about by the use of wire, trimming of the roots and branches and the restrictions placed on it by the size of the pot that it's placed in. In time, you get something completely unlike its free grown counterpart.

It was one of those days when I was struggling to cope. I was having trouble reconciling my dreams with my responsibilities. Yes, even in my old age, I struggle. I always thought that when I had time, after the children had left home, that I would be able to do some of the things that I wanted to do. I had been putting them on hold for years, waiting, but now the drought and our resources have forced me to put them on hold once again. I was sharing with a friend and anticipated their response and the response of so many people, that I should just march on and do what I want but I knew that I didn't have that in me. You see I felt like a bonsai tree.

These days we're all encouraged, ordered even, to be majestic trees. Great trees that stand tall, spread our branches out and do great things. We should produce great amounts of fruit, or shade, and/or timber for houses to be built with. Whatever tree we relate to, we are instructed to be magnificent. We live in a time when society tells us that there are no restrictions to our growth, and we can do whatever we want. All we have to do is march out there and get it.

Yet, for many of us it's not that easy. We grew up in different times and we were definitely shaped by those times. We were told that men and women had specific roles in life and while some people were brave and brash enough to defy the rules and push through those barriers, many of us didn't. Most of us, I feel, even believed that what we were told was correct and right and embraced it.

Our roots are trimmed each time we are told or remember being told that the woman's place is in the home or the man's sole role in life is to provide for his family by bringing home the bacon. Each time we remember being told that we are not capable of doing certain things or reaching a certain level of attainment. The wire of failure will stop us from reaching higher and the poor soil of the expectations of society and family will also hold us back.

Do you know what would happen to a Bonsai tree if you were to take it out of its decorative pot, cut the wire off it, plant it in good rich soil, and try to give it its freedom just as if you were untangling a bird or animal from a snare. Well, the truth is, I've been told, not much. You see, having been shaped and confined for so long means that even given the best of growing conditions it will never grow into anything like what you might expect it to.

So, I can hear you saying that we have no hope of achieving our dreams because of our past. That's not what I'm saying. When we understand that others have grown up in a different time with a different set of values, then we can understand that they may be limited in what they are able to achieve. We live in an imperfect world and even those who appear to have every opportunity and blessing will be restricted in some way or other. The message is that if someone you know appears to not be making the best of their full potential, take a step back, look at where they have come from and then see if there is some way that you can help them overcome the hurdles that *they* see in front of them, but you can't. The young people should remember that they also need to make the most of the opportunities that are available to them and embrace it. You are so very fortunate to have less restrictions than your parents or grandparents, but also remember that with those possibilities also comes great responsibility and the need to have greater compassion. A responsibility to make the most of it, to achieve good things, not bad, silly, or destructive things. Achieve your goals, make the most of your life, reach for the fame that you have within you, but do it with determination and persistence, showing grace and love towards your fellow human beings. If you do that you will become strong, powerful, and majestic just like the DNA in you determines.

There is a lot of work that goes into making any bonsai tree the way it is and they are all different. Any bonsai artist, regardless of what we think of them, considers their creation to be beautiful. The tools that are used are harsh and considered by some people to be quite brutal. If you give two Bonsai enthusiasts matching seedlings and the same equipment, you can be sure that they will come up with completely different creations. The tree doesn't ask to be treated in this way, it just happens to it, just as life happens to each of us.

When we allow God to be our craftsman, we can be confident that He will be in control and show us how these things can strengthen us, help us to grow, and develop our faith in Him, but, if we allow the devil to control our circumstances then we can expect to become ugly, distorted, and twisted. What will you choose?

Being Quarantined

When we first moved to the farm, I went from being a full-time working mum to a full-time stay-at-home mum. Not only that, I went from going to town every day to only going once a week, at most twice a week, including church. This massive change in my routine meant that I had some really bad days as we were also struggling to put food on the table for our five children and one grandchild.

At the time, my husband was working very long hours, I had three teenage girls and two small boys, and as it was twenty-five years ago, no social media. The occasional phone call was my only connection with the outside world. There were many bad days but what I learnt was that I had better days when I had a project happening.

The first project was recovering my dining room chairs, but wait, you said you didn't have enough money to feed the kids, how did you have money to recover chairs? Simple, I unpicked the covers and turned them inside out, the other side of the fabric looked much better anyway. Writing poetry was another one, getting the boys to help make a small vegetable garden, they even ate what they grew occasionally.

A few years ago, I found myself unemployed again, and one thing I started doing was taking a photo a day. This time, I did have social media to help.

In more recent times, I have found myself, again, isolated from town as the drought drained our resources and this time, knitting with stored away wool has been the thing that has kept me sane, along with my writing.

One thing I learnt over the years is that routines change, yes mostly they change slowly, but they still change. With any changes, slow or otherwise, we need to find something that will get us to think outside the box of stress.

In the early weeks, when the Covid virus managed to turn our lives upside down on a massive scale, a lot of people found their lives turned upside down but even without that, there are times when illness, accidents, or the unexpected death of a loved one will do the same thing. You will find yourself trying to come to terms with a new normal and the solution will be the same, find something to do. After the death of my mother, God gave me writing.

Now, I know everyone is different. That means that the nuts and bolts of the solution will also be different but ask God to help you find something and He will.

"For I know the thoughts that I think toward you, saith the LORD, thoughts of peace, and not of evil, to give you an expected end." Jeremiah 29:11.

One final thought, do you know what the most common phase is in the Bible? "And it came to pass...." so will this, it will not last forever, only God and our eternity in Heaven does.

Biblical Encouragers

Which Biblical people do you relate to most, who encourage you in your current circumstances?

All of us, at different times in our lives, can relate to someone in the Bible. After all, that is why their stories are recorded. They show us that they had problems, such as depression, unfaithfulness, fear, and low self-esteem. The accounts tell us that they also faced many of the life issues that we are facing today. They faced attack from enemies, droughts, floods, and famine. However, we are constantly reminded throughout the Bible of God's faithfulness to all of His people. These people were as diverse in their personalities, jobs, circumstances, and locations as you and I are today.

How About Gideon?

I had reason recently to think about what Gideon might have been feeling as he tried to feed his family by threshing grain out in a wine press. His constant struggle to feed his family in the face of the persistent bullying behaviour of the Midianites. They were constantly destroying their crops, killing their stock, and sending the Israelites into hiding. I imagine that there was also the internal pressure applied to sacrifice precious food to the false gods that the country had decided to follow. Farming was hard work and, as we know, a nation marches on its stomach. If the people are hungry, then the nation suffers.

In Australia today we can relate to this situation. In the early years of the 21st Century most of Australia had been in constant drought. Yes, there were some good years but there were far more dry years than wet. Add to that the constant changing of rules and regulations, the rise of rural crime, feral animals that destroy what little crop there is as well as our livestock, bullying tactics from animal protection and industry groups and farming in Australia doesn't seem that different to Gideon's experience.

I envisage Gideon threshing his grain and with the toss of the scoop he would be saying something like, *God, why are you not showing us your power; how long will it be before you save us?* Why do I think he did this, because its exactly what I do every time we face a change in regulations or another drought. It's the last prayer I say each night when I look outside and see stars instead of rain clouds. When I wake in the mornings and there are clear skies again, I ask: How much longer, Lord?

What Does Gideon Teach Me?

When God gives Gideon the job of saving the nation, he doesn't feel up to the task. He was a farmer/grazier. He wasn't a soldier, yet here was God calling him a mighty warrior. I think Gideon, like me, was hoping that the way out of this predicament was by using the skills that he already had.

This is just logical, and I found myself saying the same thing recently. It would be logical for me to help by using my writing and teaching skills to create a second income stream and therefore take the pressure off my husband, and yet, through the drought, the only way I was able to help was to get in the vehicle every day, drive where I didn't feel at all comfortable, get covered in dust and dirt, and then come home and catch up on my household chores.

Thus far, as I thought about Gideon, I realised that God wanted me to do something that I'm not good at, and I don't particularly like, in order to help. He gave Gideon the skills to do the job He required of him and therefore I have to trust that He will also give me the skills that I need to do the job of farming that He requires of me.

In your current circumstances, who do you find in the Bible to encourage you?

Blessings

What a wonderful sound! Rain falling on a tin roof! It is a sound that we are hearing often again now. The landscapes that we have been looking at for the last few years are now turning green. Trees we thought were dead, are recovering with green leaves poking out of bare branches.

What a blessing and we praise the Lord daily for His goodness.

Sitting in church, the preacher was talking about when Jesus fed the five thousand, and how the crowd wanted to make Him king, not because they saw Him as God to be worshipped, but because they saw him as a magical provider of their food. The same thing occurred with the woman at the well in Samarra. She initially saw Jesus' gift as a way to reduce her workload.

This struck a nerve with me, because with the rain, came a fresh load of work. Broken dam banks, damaged driveway, contour banks smashed, paddocks with water channels, weeds growing at the rate of knots, and fences flattened. As we add up the cost in dollars and hours, we feel overwhelmed by the enormity of the job in front of us.

It was tempting to ask God for a fairy godmother or the angels to come and help.

God started talking to me:

"I know what you have to do, don't I? I control time and I can make sure that you have enough of it to get through the things that need to be done."

"Remember, when I blessed Peter and John after they were fishing all night, (Luke 5:4-6, John 21:2-6)." Their workload really increased as they had to gut, salt, sell, and do whatever else was needed with all those fish, remember, it wasn't a case of catch and release.

Humbled, I remembered that not everyone has been blessed with the rain that we have seen and some have sustained greater amounts of damage than we have.

Most farmers will know the truth of Philippians 4:12-13 "I know both how to be abased, and I know how to abound: everywhere and in all things, I am instructed both to be full and to be hungry, both to abound and to suffer need. I can do all things through Christ which strengtheneth me."

Recently, someone declared they didn't understand why farmers even tried farming in Australia. The answer is simple, to answer the call of God to bless this country with food for their tables.

Blips

One day I was talking to my father on our wedding anniversary and, therefore, memories of my wedding were foremost on my mind. In particular, our wedding car, which was a black Chev, that my father bought under some interesting circumstances. Discussing it with him once, he told me that he acquired it shortly before they moved away. Since we had been married at least a year before they moved away, I was puzzled, so I sat down and actually worked out the time frames. It turned out that at ninety years old, his 'shortly' turned out to be about two years, whereas, to my perspective, even at only twenty-five years younger, shortly, to me, meant a couple of months.

Time is relative. When we are going through trials, time seems to drag on, when we are having a good time, time flies, but when we look back, both become small blips on our life screens. Yes, some are larger than others but eventually they shrink.

"For our light affliction, which is but for a moment, worketh for us a far more exceeding *and* eternal weight of glory;" 2 Corinthians 4:17

We learn the truth of the words in the Bible: "And it came to pass." God knows our limits and loves us and so He always gives us the strength and courage we need to get through life.

"There hath no temptation taken you but such as is common to man: but God *is* faithful, who will not suffer you to be tempted above that ye are able; but will with the temptation also make a way to escape, that ye may be able to bear *it*." 1 Corinthians 10:13.

While in the middle of our struggles, we should remember the most common phase in the Bible "and it came to pass" and one day our eternal life will be forever.

Buying for Survival

During the drought here in Australia so many farmers were put under enormous pressure. Charity organisations did a great job helping those who were unable to meet their basic daily needs.

However, there were many farming families that, while they can meet their daily needs, are struggling to move forward. They have other products that produce a secondary stream of income, such as craft, artwork, photos, and books, to name a few. If these products were purchased by those who generously give to charity, they would be doing so much more than they ever imagined.

Let me give you some reasons why?

It maintains the dignity of the farmers. Farmers are the last people to ask for charity. Hence, many find themselves in a position of being very desperate before they ask for help. However, if they present a product that is not dependent on rain and feed to sell, you the buyer, would be maintaining their dignity through that purchase. It's a process that has been implemented overseas and should be a method of helping our own people here in Australia.

There's a better way to give charity.

Overseas organisations are using the talents of the people to set up their own businesses so that they are able to have an ongoing income. The saying goes, 'give a man a fish and you feed him for a day, teach him to fish and he feeds himself for life', or something like that.

Sometimes, it's hard to see what is right in front of us. How could these people who produce the food that we buy in the supermarket be desperate? The food costs so much, surely they are getting the major part of the price? The truth is they don't! When you pay six dollars for a cauliflower, the farmer is most likely only getting around thirty cents. The rest of the money goes to the wholesaler, transport companies, storage facilities, and the supermarket, all making sure that they are making a profit. The farmer, however, may well be selling his stock for much less than production cost.

How do these farmers keep going? Some don't. They sell up and move on to something else, some decide that life isn't worth living, and sadly, take measures that leave their families with a whole lot of grief.

However, through it all, God sees our pain, He has promised to be with us and encourages us all to keep going, Isaiah 28:24-29 tells us that God has imparted lots of wisdom and knowledge to farmers, they know their job and their products.

Let us all be thankful that God has encouraged these people to keep going, otherwise one day we may wake up and find our supermarket shelves very empty.

Cactoblastis

In the 19th century, when prickly pear was introduced into Australia, it quickly took over, rendering much of our agricultural land useless. The industry was saved by the introduction of the Cactoblastis moth which laid its eggs on the pear and the *larvae* burrow into the pear, and eat, killing it from the inside.

While this is a good thing for our country, I cannot help thinking that it could be a reflection, on a different level, of what is happening today.

The prickly pear has spines that are part of its defence mechanism but it's no match for the destruction that goes on inside itself when the larvae hatch.

The same could be said for our country. It doesn't matter how strong or fierce we look, if the inside of our country is being destroyed, then we will be doomed anyway.

What do the Cactoblastis larvae look like for our country. Our disrespect for God and each other, wanting to look after number one first, and society last, are some of the ways in which our country is being destroyed from the inside out.

"For what shall it profit a man, if he shall gain the whole world, and lose his own soul?" Mark 8:36.

It will only be after we change our lives and decide to put the good of the country and others before personal profit and fame that our country will be able to recover from the destruction that will leave us all very vulnerable.

A return to the Biblical principles that our country was based on at Federation would be a good start.

Let nothing *be done* through strife or vainglory; but in lowliness of mind let each esteem other better than themselves. Philippians 2:3

Prayer:

Lord, please forgive my selfishness, may I put you first in my life, and by doing so, think of others first and trust you to look after the things that I need.

Call to Prayer

A news report warned of major disruptions to traffic in cities around the country as protestors demanded something be done about climate change. As a farmer's wife dealing with the effects of a drought, my only thought was that they would do a lot more good praying for rain instead of making useless demands.

Then God whispered, I've seen this all before.

1 Kings 18:25:28. "Then Elijah said to the prophets of Baal, "Since you are so numerous, choose for yourselves one bull and prepare it first. Then call on the name of your god, but do not light the fire. And they took the bull that was given them, prepared it, and called on the name of Baal from morning until noon, shouting, "O Baal, answer us!" But there was no sound, and no one answered as they leaped around the altar they had made. At noon Elijah began to taunt them, saying, "Shout louder, for he is a god! Perhaps he is deep in thought, or occupied, or on a journey. Perhaps he is sleeping and must be awakened!" So, they shouted louder and cut themselves with knives and lances, as was their custom, until the blood gushed over them."

He was right! Yes, they have changed the name of Baal to Climate Change, but the passions and the results are the same. Their Climate Change god cannot hear them or cannot give them what they want.

The day of this event began with the people of Israel being gathered together in one place.

"So, Ahab summoned all the Israelites and assembled the prophets on Mount Carmel. Then Elijah approached all the people and said, "How long will you waver between two opinions? If the LORD is God, follow Him. But if Baal is God, follow him." 1 Kings 18: 20-21.

While I know that Australia is not the new Israel, I was reminded recently we are serving the same God. God doesn't change, He may have changed the way we are able to approach Him but not His love, care, and justice.

God's people in Australia devoted the month of October to fasting and praying for rain across the whole of Australia, particularly to the drought affected parts of New South Wales, Queensland, and South Australia.

Were our prayers answered? Not straight away. Following the drought, the bushfires came but then came the rains in the form of floods which brought a new set of challenges for everyone. It's a pattern that happens time and time again in Australia. God knows that, sees us, hears our prayers, and gives us wisdom and strength each day to meet all of life's challenges.

Prayer:

God, you are a God of justice and love. You want nothing more than for all of us in Australia to love and honour you. We pray that we may hear your voice, repent our sins, and honour you, so those around us will know that you are the real creator God of the universe.

Changes

We finally managed to build new cattle yards on our property after thirty years of using the ones we had inherited. They were no longer fit for purpose. This made it necessary to pull down and dispose of the old sheep yards which had been replaced by new steel yards further out in the paddock. It was quite a process, finding many examples of hand-forged nails, gate hinges, bolts, and other pieces that we had no idea what they were designed to do.

Admiration for the workmanship that went into making the original yards, 100 plus years ago, created a conflict within me. On one hand, those yards were outdated and failing to do the job they were once designed to carry out, on the other hand, I hated to destroy such craftmanship.

I am sure that change is something that most of us have trouble coming to terms with at some time or other and at some level during our lifetime.

It would have been nice to see those yards when they were first made and in pristine condition. However, time, weather, and use had brought them to a point where they had to go. It was hard work and took weeks for us just to bring it all down. We also had to work at clearing away weeds.

Strangely, this process has had me thinking a lot about the garden of Eden. There were no weeds, things were perfect, and if man hadn't sinned, it would still be perfect, but it would have changed. Genises 2:15 says: "And the LORD God took the man, and put him into the garden of Eden to dress it and to keep it." Of course, it's hard for us to imagine what sort of work would be necessary in a perfect garden as we are so used to dealing with the things that are not perfect. The Garden of Eden was a living creation, the trees would grow, produce flowers and fruit, and as new trees would spring up under the parent tree, they would have to be moved. I am only surmising here but I have a feeling that, had the world stayed perfect, that garden would have eventually covered the whole earth. Each of Adam's children would have moved further out, however, as this is only conjecture, we don't need to waste time thinking about what if. It does give us some insight into what our reward in Heaven will be.

Revelation 21:1 says: "And I saw a new heaven and a new earth: for the first heaven and the first earth were passed away; and there was no more sea."

In the meantime, we have Jesus to help us cope and manage all the things that keep breaking and changing here. Remember, one day, if you have put your trust in Jesus, you will get to live in a perfect world forever.

Christmas

To have or not to have? This is a question.

I received a message from a friend regarding the number of pagan celebrations that took place on the 25$^{\text{th of}}$ December. There's been a lot of talk in recent years about how our Christmas is just a conversion of a pagan ritual and therefore it should be classed as pagan and not celebrated at all.

The message from my friend made me think about this whole issue a little more than I would normally do.

Firstly, even if, and there is a school of thought that says it's not, Christmas is a conversion of a pagan ritual, then it can still be celebrated because, after all, isn't that what Jesus does for us. He turns us, pagans, into people who are holy, beautiful, and acceptable to our Heavenly Father, without Jesus we are all pagans.

Secondly, it makes sense to me that if Jesus came into the world during its darkest time in history to date, then why would He not arrive at the darkest time of the year for the northern hemisphere, after all, Jesus knew that the southern hemisphere existed at the time, even if the known world had no idea. Given that there is a discrepancy of three days, this is, to me, of no consequence, given that there also appears to be a difference of three years in our dating of the years. I feel sure that God works with our humanness more than we give Him credit for.

Thirdly, I'm sure that the scholars who worked out when to hold Christmas, actually took the time to work out when Jesus arrived. We are just starting to find out that previous civilizations were, in some cases, more advanced than we are willing to give them credit for, and in some ways, more advanced than we are. The argument that the disciples didn't celebrate the birth of Jesus, and therefore we shouldn't, doesn't wash with me either. John 21:25 says, "There are also many other things which Jesus did, which if they would all be written, I suppose that even the world itself wouldn't have room for the books that would be written." I'm sure that this also applies to what the disciples did.

There was a time in our family when we celebrated Christmas in July, because we were scattered around the country, and it made it easier for us to get together then. It was a time when we were able to celebrate the birth of Jesus without all the commercial trappings and made us simplify our time together.

No matter how you feel about Christmas, the most important thing is for all of us to remember that Jesus came to earth to restore our relationship with God the Father, and you can't have the cross without His birth. Just as we shouldn't just remember His death on the cross at Easter neither should His birth only be celebrated at Christmas; we should be doing this every day of the year.

Prayer:

I thank you Lord, every day, for coming to earth, living, and dying so that our relationship with God could be restored. Amen

Coals or Fire

Winter had arrived with a sudden vengeance. There were reports of snow falling in the south of the country and in areas where snow isn't probable, the cold winds cut through us as if there was nothing holding it back.

We were so grateful that the wood stove and heater were going in order to keep us warm. I got up at five thirty in the morning to stoke them up, in order to be able to have a hot breakfast after the power had been off for whole night. Once the power had been restored, I found that we weren't quite so diligent. I came out one morning to notice that both the heater and stove had gone out overnight.

However, on investigation, I found that there were enough hot coals to make it come to life easily, I just had to uncover them, fuel them, and encouraged them into life.

As I uncovered the coals, I couldn't help thinking that things, such as covid isolation, stress of drought, and then flood damage, and general busyness, had caused my spiritual life to be buried, causing it to lose its fire.

I'm sure that it happens to others as well and can sometimes hit us unexpectedly, or it may creep up on us unnoticed.

In order to have our fire reignited, we need some encouragement, refueling, in order to be effective. Not just from scripture but from those around us.

Do you know someone who could use some help to get back on fire for the Lord?

"Wherefore comfort yourselves together, and edify one another, even as also ye do." 1Thessalonians 5:11.

Ask the Lord, to help you uncover them, encourage, and refuel them. That may be the greatest thing you could do for someone, and the Lord, as many try to find their way back in the particularly difficult times that we have experienced in the last few years and it will be needed even more as we face more difficult times ahead.

"Now the God of patience and of encouragement grant you to be of the same mind one with another according to Christ Jesus," Romans 15:5.

Prayer:

Lord, show us those who need to be encouraged today. Give us the courage to spend some time and encourage them so that they may stay on fire for you.

Common is Special

A friend placed some of what she called *common geraniums* in a crystal vase, making a beautiful picture. I have to say that my first reaction was to feel a bit sorry for these very bright flowers. Yes, they grow easily without needing too much attention, they can be propagated without too much trouble, yet their beauty fills many gardens with colour, particularly where the owners are time poor.

I immediately thought about us as common humans. You know, the ones that don't achieve great things in the eyes of men or struggle to be different to the many? Most of us fall into the category of being common or ordinary.

Yet, when God places us, and He does, in His crystal vase through the blood of Jesus we make a very big difference to someone's world. That world might not extend beyond our front gate or our small town, but just like those geraniums that brighten up a small room, we make a big difference right where we are.

Mark 5:18-20 tells of a man Jesus healed who wanted to travel the country with Him, but what did Jesus tell him to do? Go home to your own people and tell them. While we are not told what happened after that, we can only imagine what a difference he might have been able to make in his home village.

Like the common geranium, we don't last very long, but while we are here, let's make sure that we brighten the world in which we have been placed and remember, that because we have been placed in a crystal vase, the effect will be greater as we work for our Father, not in our own strength, but in His.

Isaiah 41:10 "Don't you be afraid, for I am with you. Don't be dismayed, for I am your God. I will strengthen you. Yes, I will help you. Yes, I will uphold you with the right hand of my righteousness."

Confusion

I had been going through an extended period of internal confusion. The rest of the world was in a state of disorder, but I was a Christian, and therefore, my life should be calm and meaningful despite the external environment. I just didn't know what God wanted me to do that would be substantial for Him. This internal battle, at times, even made me doubt my salvation. I lived on a farm, where very few people came to visit, and even less came after the Covid 19 lockdowns were lifted. How could I reach people for Him if I never saw anyone? I described my feelings to someone as being stuck in a small space surrounded by a hedge and I was constantly walking around this space looking for a way out but there didn't appear to be one.

After talking to another person, I realized that I was running on spiritual empty. I hadn't had a lot of deep fellowship since the death of my mother, which at the time, was eight years earlier. Over the next year, I started to do some things around the house, painting, remodeling of some furniture pieces, cleaning, and clearing things, which made me feel better about my house and I learnt how to do a lot of things that I would never have been game to try a few years before, but it still felt pointless.

I agreed with Soloman in Ecclesiastes 1:2-3

"Vanity of vanities, saith the Preacher, vanity of vanities; all *is* vanity. What profit hath a man of all his labour which he taketh under the sun?"

If I was putting all this work into something that could be taken away from me in a heartbeat, what was the point in doing it in the first place. I know that I'm not the first person to think like this, there are many others who think the same way.

Then one morning, I was listening to "Jesus Came to Save Sinners" by Charles Spurgeon and he said one very simple thing, "The devil means to drive you to despair by such thoughts or at least keep you from trusting Jesus."

It was such a simple thing, but in that moment, I realised that all my confusion was not about working out what God wanted me to do but it was all about keeping me from trusting God.

Yes, all the things that I have done might be meaningless, in that they could be undone in a split second, but that shouldn't destroy my trust in God, He will hold my hand while I continue to live with Him and ultimately take me home to Heaven.

"Behold, I have engraved you on the palms of my hands. Your walls are continually before me." Isaiah 49:16.

"Even there your hand will lead me, and your right hand will hold me." Psalm 139:10.

No matter what is happening, even inside us, God has us and just wants us to trust Him.

Country Roads

How do you cope with the different types of roads that you might drive on?

I've been driving for around 45 years now, and I am pleased to say, thanks to the grace of God, that I've only had one accident, hit one wild animal, and been pulled over twice for speeding.

The accident was recent, and some people asked how I was managing on the road. Was I very nervous? Well surprisingly, no. On the sealed roads and even our gravel or dirt roads I was, and am, really quite okay driving. While driving, you might find me talking to the Lord, and even singing. It's all part of my time with God, quite relaxed and informal. We have a great time together.

Now, you would think that if I was okay on the roads that I would be okay driving around the paddock feeding sheep. Here is the thing though, I'm not! You see, I am a formed-road driver. Put me in the paddock, with rocks, dips, gullies, and uneven terrain and I become a blubbering mess. Four-wheel driving is not a pastime that I am the least bit interested in taking up. For months, we had to do this activity everyday while feeding our sheep through the drought. You might think that the more I did this, the easier it would be, WRONG! Now, this is where you find my conversations with God having a completely different tone. My prayers are formal, desperate, and cries for help, strength, and courage. We don't have such a great time together.

Isn't this like our lives though.

When times are good, smooth, and reasonably stress free. Our conversations with God are ones of praise and singing. We are relaxed and informal with our Lord and friend.

However, when troubles roll in, and they do with monotonous regularity, our conversations with God have a very different purpose and tone. These are the times when we find ourselves pleading for protection, crying for strength and courage to get through the trials and to stay faithful.

Without both of these types of journeys, life would be dull. The rough patches teach us about the faithfulness of our Lord, and the smooth ways show us the abundant grace that he stows upon us.

But the God of all grace, who hath called us unto his eternal glory by Christ Jesus, after that ye have suffered a while, make you perfect, stablish, strengthen, settle *you*. 1 Peter 5:10.

Do you thank God for all the different roads you have travelled on?

Covered

I was clearing out some weeds between bricks that formed a small courtyard in my garden. If it had been done properly there shouldn't have been any weeds to get rid of. As I pulled, some weeds came out easily, others were harder, and some were too hard to remove.

I was reminded about our lives. We live in a fallen world, like that courtyard, it's no longer perfect. As Christians, God's word and love covers us, just as the bricks cover the ground that produces the weeds that grew up through the cracks, so some sins invade our lives no matter how hard we try to live according to the word of God.

But here is where the good news arrives, most of those weeds/sins are much easier to remove, simply because God's love helps us on a daily basis to get rid of them. However, we should be aware that there will always be some that are harder to remove while ever we are living on this side of Heaven.

This doesn't mean that we should stop praying and give up, I've heard of some people who will not even acknowledge that they have sins, or if they do they blame their genetic makeup and refuse to even try to correct their behaviour. The grace of God is always available to help us even if, at times, we slip into old habits more times than we care to.

"For now, we see in a mirror, dimly, but then face to face. Now I know in part, but then I will know fully, even as I was also fully known." 1 Corinthians 13:12.

Prayer:

God, I thank you that you love covers me every day and teaches me about what is right and wrong in my life. Amen

Dare to be a....

Have you ever been laughed at for doing something? How did it make you feel? Did you feel so bad that you actually stopped doing what was close to your heart? Or were you so committed to the project that you found the courage to keep going, even in the face of the laughter and jeering?

I remember a Sunday School song, 'Dare to be a Daniel'. It's meant to inspire us to stand up for what we believe is right in the face of opposition.

As we struggled through the worst drought that Australia has seen in the life of European settlement, many people came up with solutions that could help farmers cope. Yet, many were not even considered as viable solutions because of the fear of being laughed at. Yet, if we can solve the problems our farmers face, we would be able to help other countries faced with similar problems. God gave us brains to solve the problems that we are presented with, not only that, but He also promises to help and inspire us. Our country has a history of droughts and floods, yet we fail to save the flood water in order to assist the farmers during dry times. We don't 'Dare to be a Noah'.

There was someone else who was most likely laughed at for doing something that he knew he had been called to do in order to save others. He might have saved a great deal more people if only they had believed in his solution. Yes, if Noah was laughed at because

God had given him a project to build it didn't cause him to down tools, he kept going and met all the challenges during the many years that it took to complete the Ark.

I was thinking over these things the other day and I suddenly realized that if Noah had succumbed to the pressure to give up, we would not be here, we would no longer exist.

Yes, I understand that, theologically, God would have found someone else to build that Ark or another way to save humanity, because God is so patient with us. However, it made me wonder!

So, if you are being laughed at for doing something that you feel sure God has planted on your heart, 'Dare to be a Noah' and keep on going. God has a very special reason for you to be part of the plan and He will complete His plan, not only for you but for the rest of the world.

Prayer:

Lord, your word tells us that life here on earth will not be easy. Yet, we fail to be like Noah and continue to carry on no matter how hard things are. Give us the strength to use the brains that you have given us to improve things, not only for ourselves, but for all of humanity. Amen

Dividing our Country

As we watched the election campaign from the comfort of our lounge room, we were horrified at the nasty behaviour by some of those involved. We shook our heads and wondered how our country, known all around the world for being fair and willing to help the underdog, had managed to fall to such levels of social disunity. The contrast was even more stark when, on the death of Bob Hawke, a previous Prime Minister, they ran back flashes of life in Australia then. Oh, what has made us so competitive that we would stoop to such dirty strategies.

A few days after the election, having had my fill of post-election news media commentary, I looked for something enjoyable to watch while I ate my breakfast. I found a documentary on people who had built homes in the USA that met and overcame the challenges of their environments. It showed how these people worked together, innovated, and achieved their ultimate dream homes. As it finished, a rerun of the Block came on, an Australian program where people renovate homes, and I was hit with a feeling of despair, I just wanted to turn it off. Why? The question hung there for a while. It was still about innovation and building dream places to live, so why did I find it so unpleasant.

The answer came quickly enough. The first show, even though things were tough, proved that with hard work and co-operation great things could be achieved. The second was about the competition and winning, not necessarily at any cost, but winning none the less.

This made me reflect on the election campaign again. One team promoted winning and getting what you could for yourself, the other, working together and helping each other to make this country what it could be again.

Which brings me to the subtle things that are working to divide this country. With the proliferation of reality tv shows, there is very little else on, certainly on free tv in regional areas, the constant message that is unconsciously being sent out is that everything is a competition. We must win to achieve and reach the top. Of course, this is not the only way this message is being sent out in order to try and divide this country, but it was one that was provided the strong contrast for me as I watched that day.

Well, for the first time in a long time, Scott Morrison and his team who promoted working together, proved this message to be very wrong.

So, let's be aware of the underlying messages that are being sent to us, via not only our tv shows but other forms of media, and start remembering that by working together we achieve a lot more than by competing against each other.

We are a diverse country, in backgrounds, talents, and skills. God created us to work together side by side, not just as male and female but as a team.

"And the LORD God said, *It is* not good that the man should be alone; I will make him an help meet for him." Genesis 2:18.

"From whom the whole body fitly joined together and compacted by that which every joint supplieth, according to the effectual working in the measure of every part, maketh increase of the body unto the edifying of itself in love." Ephesians 4:16.

Prayer:

Lord, may we all see through the subtle messages that would try to break the bonds between us as human beings. Help us to see them for what they are and engage the enemy by forging stronger relationships with each other, knowing that all of us have important skills that are needed to make this country a better place in which to live.

Don't Let the Cat Out

Once, in an interview, I asked that people pray that farmers have enough courage to carry out their daily duties during a long drought. Now, I've realized that we need to pray for everyone to have courage.

We are not the first generation to live in a society where the governments have implemented laws that are contrary to the laws of God. It's much easier to let the cat out of the bag than to put it back in afterwards. In other words, once the laws allow us to go against God's word, it's a lot harder, nearly impossible, to change to laws back so that we are again aligned with the Word of God. The Old Testament is not a book of stories but a record of real events.

In *Turning Water into Wine*, I wrote a story about people needing to pray on their feet. Praying on our feet requires courage, because it means that we pray while we are doing the things that God wants us to carry out.

Nehemiah is a wonderful example of praying on your feet. He needed courage to ask the King for something that was very important to him but could also have had him beheaded just for feeling miserable about the state of Jerusalem.

Daniel, Shadrach, Meshach, and Abednego all had to live during a time when the law of the land was against their faith and an abomination to the Lord. Yet, they prayed to God and had the courage to defy the law. Just like us, once the laws have been passed, there is little we can do about them except to pray that people will have the courage to defy them.

How? You ask.

Pray that people have the courage to say no when an abortion is recommended, even when the baby is not wanted by the birth parents. To not take revenge when they are wronged. The courage to be quiet when someone is rude to them. The courage to stick to their own convictions when others around them are ridiculing them. Most of all, pray for those in authority, it's so easy to complain but much harder to shut our mouth, bow our heads, and pray that God will help them to make good choices for our town, state, and country.

Encouraging Others

Encouragement can lift people higher than we will ever know. It comes in so many different forms. Once, when I didn't ring my father for Father's Day until nearly nine in the evening, he told me that if I had forgotten, which I nearly did, it would have been the first time. I got off the phone determined that I would never forget again, even though I wasn't aware that I hadn't forgotten any of the important days in their lives.

We live in a world that dishes out discouragement far too often and in very high volumes. The consequences of this are that many people, unable to put such criticism aside, end up feeling despondent.

God has led me to write in such a way as to encourage people in small doses. No long stories where you must remember where the story line was up to, just long enough to have with a cuppa and capable of giving the reader a boost of reassurance.

I am surprised at the way God has used my writing. Once a man read my story, 'Balancing Act' and God used it to help him change a lightbulb. Yes, something as small as that. Another reader read the story, 'Standing Up' which encouraged them to keep going through some very tough times.

Someone else had a good laugh over the story of a horse painted with whitewash and another loved the story about the Three Wells.

This sort of feedback tells me that there are many more people out there who could be helped if only they were able to get a copy of my book.

You, my readers, know many people yourselves who need such encouragement.

There is a very simple way for you to help them get such benefits and it won't mean that you must buy volumes of my books either.

Just recommend my book to your friends whom you know could use a boost up in times of need, if they ask their local library to get it in, they win.

Of course, this is not the only way to encourage those that need it, a smile, kind word, or just a listening ear, may be all that you need to do.

I Thessalonians 5:11 says: Wherefore comfort yourselves together, and edify one another, even as also ye do.

Eternity is a long time.

Farming is a way of life that includes many times of high activity and focus, for instance, when shearing or harvest is happening, everyone is expected to be on deck and functioning in order to make sure that the job is completed in a certain time frame. These events don't just last for a day or two but often for weeks on end. All of life's other jobs have to still be dealt with in and around the shearing or harvest, they can't take a back seat or be put on hold, so life is busy, very busy, and people often get tired and overwhelmed.

At one shearing, I was tired, and feeling frustrated as I listed the amount of work that needed to be done, when suddenly, I remembered with a thankful heart that shearing would be finished in two days' time. We would finally be able to take a breath and have a few days of down time before the next round, whatever that would be. Farming is like that; you never know what is around the next corner.

God spoke to my heart, just be grateful that the end is in sight, imagine what it would be like if that was never going to happen. Oh, Lord, how hard is it going to be for those who don't love you. For those who go to hell for eternity, there will never be a break, no down time for them.

There is only one way for those we love to avoid this type of eternity, and that is to trust Jesus, to get to know Him.

Our job is not only to pray for these people, but to tell them that there will be a better life after this one, but it comes at a price, the price that Jesus paid on the cross, so that we don't regret our choices forever.

Romans 10:14 says, "How then will they call on him in whom they have not believed? How will they believe in him whom they have not heard? How will they hear without a preacher?"

Are you telling those around you about the power of God to save them, not just by the way you are living, but by praying and using every opportunity to tell them that Jesus loves them?

Fellowship

It was Sunday morning and we had decided to only attend church online. Someone posted the next day asking about how to allow God to lead you if you found church hard to attend.

One friend reminded me that the church were the hands and feet of Jesus, something I had pushed to the back of my mind, and I think many of us do the same from time to time. We get so caught up in the logistics of what we are told what we need to do, that we forget to ask God what He wants us to do as individuals.

We are the church, we are the hands and feet of Christ, there are a couple of children's songs that teach them this, but its easily forgotten as we grow older.

However, what I have learnt over the last few years when we weren't able to go to church during Covid19 is that we need to make sure that we have fellowship with at least someone. This is something that Paul knew was important for us when he wrote to the Hebrews "not forsaking our own assembling together, as the custom of some is, but exhorting one another, and so much the more as you see the Day approaching." (10:25).

While I was spending time with my sister, I realised that I had a period of eight years where I didn't have this special fellowship, which had left me not only feeling confused, but lost about my spiritual life. During the previous year, I had found the work that I carried out for the Lord, just sheer hard work and I had lost my joy in living. There are many ways to be locked down but when we ask God to bring fellowship into our lives, He will answer that prayer in ways that we will not expect because He knows just how important it is for our growth.

Do you have someone that you can share with?

Following the Rules

I've been doing some knitting for a few years. I started in order to try and relax and found that my skills were getting better, so once we opened the shop, we placed a few extra items I had in the window and then people started to ask me to knit some things for them.

One particular pattern for a jacket was new to me, but didn't seem to be very difficult and I started out full of confidence that I could manage it. The first row worked great I thought, but then the second row was a stitch short. I made an adjustment and carried on. It wasn't until I started knitting the left side of the jacket that I realized that I wasn't doing exactly what the pattern required. I had made an assumption that meant the work was one stitch short all the way up the right front of this jacket. This meant a re-knit of the whole right side again, which was fine as I wasn't on a tight schedule to have it finished. I made some adjustments to the pattern to make it more acceptable for the client and moved on. It turns out that she was happy with the finished product, and I just unraveled the incorrect part and knitted it into another jacket.

I wonder how many times, when we ask God for things, we also make some assumptions, not big ones, maybe that the answers to our prayers should look a certain way, for instance you might need a certain job done and your prayer is that God will send you the money so you can pay someone to do it for you, and yet the answer

God has for you is that he will give you the courage to be able to do it yourself.

'Let's therefore draw near with boldness to the throne of grace, that we may receive mercy and may find grace for help in time of need.' Hebrews 4:16.

If I had read the instruction properly in the first place, I wouldn't have needed to start that project over again, and yes, sometimes, because we expect God to answer in a particular manner, we end up having more work to do.

It's not an easy thing to do, but let's pray and then wait until God answers in His own way, which in the end might save us extra work.

From Rock to Rock

The LORD is my rock, my fortress and my deliverer; my God is my rock, in whom I take refuge, my shield and the horn of my salvation, my stronghold.

As we visited the Nativity again one year, I was struck by something that I hadn't noticed before. We accept that Jesus was born in a stable, but do we consider that the stable may not have been a modern construction? It is likely to have been a cave, a natural hollowed-out rock, repurposed to shelter animals from storms. If we accept this, then we can also note that His earthly life ended inside a rock, closed for a short time and opened again by the power of God. 1 Corinthians 10:4 says: and all drank the same spiritual drink. For they drank of a spiritual rock that followed them, and the rock was Christ.

Suddenly, God's saving power coming from a rock took on a new dimension for me. There are so many times in scripture where life comes from a rock. How can that be? Rocks are lifeless, solid, too hard for anything to grow out of and, on a farm, they can be dangerous and yet twice the Israelites received lifesaving water from a rock, the first time during their first year of exile (Exodus 17:6) God tells Moses to strike the rock and the second time (Numbers 20:8-11) when Moses was to speak to the rock, for the people to be saved.

On other occasions, prophets are told to hide in the rock to save themselves, David lived in caves as protection from Saul.

So, are we surprised that the birthplace of Jesus actually took place in a cave, a rock that provided protection for the Son of God? Does it astonish us that He would begin His life on earth in exactly the same type of dwelling it would end in?

So, why would this be important? Who cares about this sort of detail in the line of history? For me, it's another assurance that God is faithful, what He begins, He finishes, in exactly the way He began it. When He created the world, He also created the very place from which He would enter the world and his final resting place. This reminds me that God is interested in the finest details of history, His, yours, mine, and the world's.

If He is interested in these small details for His journey on Earth, then He is also interested in the minute details of your history, my history, and because He is faithful, each detail of our lives has been taken care of.

God's Care in Dry Times

It had been a few weeks of lots of stress. It had been weeks since it had rained, the ground was so dry, I felt alone, overwhelmed, and about as dry as the ground outside.

There were some jobs that I just couldn't manage on my own, no matter which way I looked at them. The plan was to move furniture around in order to make room for our grandson to move in with us. I just had to wait until he was ready to move in and he would have to help, but somehow, I had a feeling that would be a lot of extra drama I didn't want. Other family members were so busy with their own lives and the extra work that comes with drought conditions. I would wait but each time I walked past them I mentally shook my head.

A friend arrived with her arm in plaster. I explained that the mess was a result of waiting to get these jobs done. She wanted to see what I was planning and said that she would help. I protested because of her arm but she declared that it wouldn't stop her as she was doing most things anyway. She had a cuppa and indicated that she was keen to get started.

A couple of hours later, the furniture was moved into their new positions with very little drama, and she went on her way. Thankful, I praised God for sending my gracious friend.

A couple of days later, I was really stressed and on my way to town to see a doctor, when I noticed my car was behaving strangely. I pulled over and got out to find that a flat tyre was the cause. I was too far from home to turn around to get help from the men working at the shed. The nearby house was deserted. Well, I couldn't sit there and wait for someone to come, this was a backroad. Had it been the morning or later in the evening there was a chance of someone coming along as they travelled to or from work, but not now. There was nothing for it, I had to do this by myself. It was the middle of the day and hot. Thank goodness the doctor hadn't given me a specific time to be there. They were going to fit me in when they could after I arrived.

Again, I said to the Lord, it just you and me! I'm going to need your help here because I'm pretty sure I'm not strong enough to get those nuts off. I had just gotten the stuff out of the boot, (or trunk), and started when I heard a vehicle coming. A neighbour's grandson pulled up and quickly finished the job for me. Thanking the Lord, I got to town and completed my jobs which now included getting a new tyre.

And so here I was, hanging washing out two days later. The sound of dripping water reached me. In a drought, wasting water is an absolute crime. Having found the source of the noise, I looked at how I could stop the dripping but found that the tap couldn't be turned off. A tree had actually grown around the tap making it impossible to move the handle.

My first thought was that at least the tree was getting the much-needed water at a time when it just didn't rain.

I realised that if we wrap ourselves around the sources of our strength (God), like the tree had wrapped itself around the source of water, there was no way that His love and care can be turned off. God had shown me that during the week.

Can you remember times when God has cared for you during tough times?

God has the Reins.

As a child, did you ever watch one of those movies where someone is on a horse or in a vehicle and it is racing towards a cliff. You probably held your breath, expecting them to go over and relaxed when the horse or vehicle stopped just short, or turned away from the precipice just in time.

Later, when you watched the same movie again, maybe you had to keep telling yourself that they would not go over, you know that because you've seen it all before, but sometimes it's easy to still feel relieved when the outcome actually is the same as your memory told you it would be.

By the time you become an adult, you have seen so many movies that you can sit there and say, they have to stop or turn in time otherwise the story wouldn't work.

In life, we often find ourselves in situations where time is of the essence. Maybe you have to find somewhere to live before the date of your current lease is over, or some other job has to be completed before a certain deadline, but you are dependent on other people or things to happen before it can be completed. In other words, it wouldn't matter how hard you work, things are not going to be ready if these other issues are not solved in time. God's intervention is the only way things are to be done.

You can't see the solutions and that deadline, or cliff is coming up fast.

However, even though you know that God has been faithful so many times before, it's easy to wonder if things are going to work out this time. It's hard not to cry out and say but this time it's different, which is true, most likely, however what is difficult to remember is that God's story has to work out in the way He wants. This means He knows everything about your story. He knew the beginning, the middle and the end, because he wrote it, which also means that He has the answer.

Psalm 139 reminds us that God knows all about us, and Revelation 22:13 says, I am the Alpha and the Omega, *the* Beginning and *the* End, the First and the Last."

Yes, often it looks as if the cliff is coming up fast and while it is hard, we need to rest in the knowledge that God already has the answer.

God is NOT Surprised

A couple we knew were devastated to learn that they were to become first time grandparents. In their eyes, the parents-to-be were too young and should have waited until they were more settled before having children. As I prayed for the family, there were a few things that came to mind.

They are not the first people to have to deal with this issue. Many parents have had to deal with it, all the way down through history. Many families have been torn apart because there has been a lack of acceptance and in the past, many parents have been forced to put their child up for adoption because of the lack of support causing a lot of heartache for the rest of their lives.

"The thing that hath been, it *is that* which shall be; and that which is done *is* that which shall be done: and *there is* no new *thing* under the sun." Ecclesiastes 1:9.

While these and many other parents are surprised by this sort of news, God is never surprised, He knew about this child and many others from before the beginning of time. Jeremiah 1:5 says: Before I formed thee in the belly, I knew thee; and before thou camest forth out of the womb I sanctified thee, *and* I ordained thee a prophet unto the nations." If God knew and had a plan for Jeremiah, He also knows and has a plan for everyone, and that not only applies to you and me, but to all those who are born in the future, planned or otherwise. God knows them all.

No one knows what the future might hold for any of us, and there have been many couples who have waited only to find that there were medical issues that needed to be overcome, which might have been solved had the treatment started earlier. I also thought about the many parents who accepted and supported their children and found later in life that they were very blessed by the care shown to them by these special grandchildren.

No matter how surprised you are by any sort of news you receive today, know that God is not surprised, He knew all about this before time began, even your surprise. We are all that special to Him.

God's Calling

Both my parents we committed Christians all their lives, so being born to these parents, who were both very good examples of how to walk in the way Jesus wants us to go, was a privilege. In one sense it was an advantage, but it also makes it hard for me to determine when exactly I became a Christian. I remember coming home for lunch one day, during fifth year of schooling, and telling mum that I had made a decision to follow Jesus personally. However, if you were to ask me for a date and time, I couldn't pin it down.

I always believed that God would lead me into ministry, just as my parents were, which He has, but it's a very different looking ministry.

Did my life change dramatically after that lunchtime confession of faith? No, not really, however, all through my life I have walked through green valleys and dry places, and the Holy Spirit has been there with me every step of the way. The green valleys were times when I could see the Holy Spirit doing special things in my life, such as being part of an outreach organization at high school, my first year away from home working and having fellowship with new Christian friends. The training I received during this period of my life led me to believe that I would eventually enter the ministry.

My mother had married a minister and ended up farming and I have to admit that I often thought that I would do the reverse, I married a farmer and expected to end up in the ministry.

My marriage to a farmer in 1978, meant that my life took a path that called me to minister to my husband's family, none of whom had heard the word of God. Through much prayer and witnessing in what were challenging circumstances, we have seen at least one member of this family come to Christ before he was called home. As for the other members, we wait until judgement day to see if they made the right choice before they ran out of time. In this role, God was to teach me many and varied lessons about unconditional love, perseverance, tolerance, and using his imagination not only to train and care for the five children that God gave us, each one with different health and personality challenges, but also to find unique solutions to everyday problems. I used what I had at hand, and repurposed things, such as using a tablecloth for curtain pelmet, and a bassinet for a toy box. These are just a few of the solutions He helped me to find. Through His grace I was able to find work outside the home and undertake my teacher training during the many years that interest rates were high and we were in the process of buying our farm. He provided a live-in babysitter, who not only helped us out, but we were able to provide a safe place for them while they were with us.

His greatest miracle was in allowing me to give birth to our two boys. After three girls and six miscarriages I was led to believe that I would never be able to have a son. Something I wanted badly. His guiding hand took me to a Naturopath, who was able to diagnose several mineral deficiencies which, once corrected, not only allowed me to successfully have two sons, but increased my energy levels and put an end to my panic attacks.

Through a minister I was encouraged to write for our church bulletin, which looking back, was the start of my writing journey and ministry through books.

He does His most powerful work through me every day, helping me to get out of bed when I don't feel I want to, when I am aching all over, when I'm depressed, and I don't want to face the stress of farming life. He helps me do things around the farm, giving extra strength and courage when I need it. It's in the mundane things of life that I see His most powerful work. It is these experiences that form the basis of my stories.

Sometimes, I still struggle with my calling, my ministry. I dreamed of being a preacher like my parents, instead, I have been called to minister through written words.

Isaiah 55:8-9 reminds us that God doesn't think the same way we do. "For my thoughts *are* not your thoughts, neither *are* your ways my ways, saith the LORD. For *as* the heavens are higher than the earth, so are my ways higher than your ways, and my thoughts than your thoughts."

My first book came about almost accidentally, a series of stories written for the church bulletin and used as encouragement for others. When I realized that I had written enough for a book, I decided it was time. After this I kept writing, and the books kept coming. In 2019, my daughter and I started our own publishing group as it was becoming too expensive to publish externally, and, while I still wonder what God is doing, I know that He has blessed people through, not only my books, but the other books we have published as well.

In what ways has God's calling for you been different to the way you imagined it? Thank Him for doing things differently.

God's Quiet Voice

One night, as I tried to sleep, I heard the neighbour's cows calling for their calves. The owner must have separated them during the day. The tone is one of distress and while they are a long way away the noise carries across the miles on the night air. The separation is made in order to allow the calves to grow stronger and the cows to recover from feeding their offspring. In the morning, the noise was even louder, the cows sounding very close to panicked.

As I listened, the similarity with our lives in a world trying to deal with a pandemic wasn't lost on me. They sounded just like many of the people we talked to and the news feeds on our social media and television sets.

But closer to home I hear another voice, a bird is singing. It's quieter and relaxed, it's enjoying the cool morning air. What I discovered was that when I focused on the bird song, the noise of the cattle faded, if I focused on the cattle and their cries the bird song faded.

In a world in distress, I need to remember to stay focused on the voice that is calm, relaxed, and reassuring. That voice belongs to God, our Lord!

I was reminded of the time when Elijah felt that he was alone. It's very easy for us to feel alone these days, even now that we are no longer locked in our homes. What did God tell Elijah to do?

"Then He said, "Go out, and stand on the mountain before the LORD." And behold, the LORD passed by, and a great and strong wind tore into the mountains and broke the rocks in pieces before the LORD, *but* the LORD *was* not in the wind; and after the wind an earthquake, *but* the LORD *was* not in the earthquake; And after the earthquake a fire; *but* the LORD *was* not in the fire: and after the fire a still small voice".

The voice asked Elijah what he is doing. Now I know that we cannot go out and literally stand before a mountain, not unless you live on a farm somewhere that has one, you cannot run the risk of being arrested. We are already standing in front of a mountain anyway, even in our homes. While we are there let us remember that God's voice is the quiet one, the bird over the cows, and He is speaking to us, we just need to stay focused in order to keep hearing Him.

"God *is* faithful, by whom you were called into the fellowship of His Son, Jesus Christ our Lord."

At a time when face to face fellowship with other humans is at an all-time low, let us remember that Jesus, through the Holy Spirit, can share with us at anytime, anywhere, and use even cows and birds to speak to us.

Prayer:

Lord, help us to hear your voice of reassurance in the quiet things. Help us to focus on you and place the panic in the background where it belongs. Remind us constantly that you are in control and that all these trials will help our faith to grow stronger as long as we stay focused on you. Amen.

God's Teaching

First, there was the drought! We had to learn to be careful with our water and food. Next the bushfires, to teach us to be careful with our environment and then there was the pandemic, teaching us to be careful with our health.

It might be just the teacher in me, but I see an up grading of the lessons here on a global scale. Each lesson is a little more difficult and affects more people. We, as individuals, were being taught the lessons inside a very large classroom.

Yet, God still says to us, in the same way he spoke to Joshua all those years ago, "Have I not commanded you? Be strong and of good courage; do not be afraid, nor be dismayed, for the LORD your God *is* with you wherever you go." Joshua 1:9.

Remember, this young man had been helping Moses for years, he wasn't just dropped in at the deep end, as we say, he had been in training for a long time, and yet, it seems when the time came for him to step up and take on the leader's role, he was feeling very alone and unqualified. Why do I think this? Well, God had to tell him three times (Joshua 1: 5,6 and 9) in a short space of time to be strong and courageous.

During the pandemic all of us had to cope with things that we had never done before. Home schooling children, working from home, not being able to go shopping when we felt like it, even just staying at home all day every day was a challenge to most of us and while this happened then on a global scale, it still happens in the lives of most people at some point during their lifetime. Everyone will, at some time or other, find that they need to meet challenges that we never imagined would be on our radar.

Yet, God is saying to His people, His leaders, His family, the same thing that He said to Joshua.

"Have I not commanded you? Be strong and of good courage; do not be afraid, nor be dismayed, for the LORD your God *is* with you wherever you go."

Learning to trust Him in all the circumstances we face is the overall lesson, that same lesson runs through all that happens to us and will continue to run through any new lessons that He might want us to have.

I claim this promise, for any time of tribulation and look forward to Him being glorified soon and you can claim it too. "And unless those days were shortened, no flesh would be saved; but for the elect's sake those days will be shortened." Matthew 24:22.

God will not let our trials go on forever because He knows how frail we are, after all He made us, and that makes us very precious to Him.

Grounded

Did your parents ground you when you were younger as punishment for breaking some rule or other? It's a common method of trying to get us to think about the choices we have made and gives us time to resolve to make better decisions in the future.

I found, when I grounded my kids, there were usually two reactions. They either used the time to do something that they wanted to do at home or fumed and moaned.

So, when we become adults, we usually think that we can put away the fear of 'being grounded' again. We, maybe think that we have learnt those lessons and trust that we'll make more mature decisions.

So, does God ground us?

God is our loving Father. He always wants the best for us. Yet, it is harder to listen to Him. There are so many other voices around us all the time. These come in the form of what others think we should be doing. It doesn't matter how they give the message, it often drowns out the voice that we should be listening to, that of our loving God.

There was a time when I found myself grounded.

How?

I wrecked my car when I hit a 4X4 at a roundabout in town while I was driving home. I praise God every day for my safety and that I didn't sustain any injuries. The other vehicle bore no noticeable damage. Living 20 minutes' drive out of town makes it too far to walk anywhere. So, unless my husband is able to go to town, I was grounded. I'm too short to drive his ute.

What struck me as a little funny, was that very morning I had been discussing the need to have some repairs carried out and had declared to my husband, "My car is indispensable".

What is God trying to teach me?

Lesson One

Never say that you cannot do without a material item. God will show us that the only thing that is indispensable on this earth is Him. He will always provide a way for us to get what we need. On two occasions, a friend has paid us a visit on the same day as our papers arrive in town and has been willing to bring them out to us.

The Good News Translation puts Psalm 16:5 this way: "You, LORD, are all I have, and you give me all I need; my future is in your hands".

Lesson Two

Think ahead. Be well-organized. When I had access to town, via my car, it didn't matter if I forgot something. All I had to do was get back in the car, usually the next day and pick up what I'd forgotten. So, it is important for me to now make lists, checking it twice before we take a trip to town in my husband's ute.

However!

It appeared that I wasn't learning these lessons fast enough. A week later, I hurt my foot helping my husband cart water to our stock. Again, I was blessed to not break any bones, but walking was painful. So, I now needed to make sure that I did not waste my steps around the house.

Blessed.

God has given me some 'Time Out'. I can thank him that has allowed me to finish a commissioned knitting piece and some editing for a new book to be released in early September to help my sister and I to honour our mother.

"If ye then, being evil, know how to give good gifts unto your children, how much more shall your Father which is in heaven give good things to them that ask him?" Matthew 7:11.

Has God ever grounded you? Did you learn lessons during that time, or did you fume and moan?

Growth in the Dark

Between wet weather and other major jobs, we left the garden to its own devices for a considerable amount of time.

As with all these things, mowing the yard finally managed to reach the top of the list. Warm and wet conditions meant that the grass was long. So, once the grass was cut there were some works around the edges that needed to be carried out. I tackled these jobs in small stages to make things look respectable for Christmas. During that process, I discovered, under a heap of grass, a plant that had flowered. So, what is remarkable about that? This plant only flowers in winter, and here we were in the middle of December which in Australia means it is the middle of summer.

The tall strands of grass kept it cool and dark enough to trick it into thinking it was still winter.

As I looked at the flower, I thought about how we are living in dark times. Just as the plant managed to flower in the dark, so many of us are continuing to grow behind the dark headlines and struggles of a broken world.

Even though the world cannot see the beauty and growth that God brings to our lives during our dark times, it still exists. He can see it and He rejoices in it.

"For nothing is hidden, that will not be revealed; nor anything secret, that will not be known and come to light" Luke 8:17.

The world puts so much emphasis on being visible. Even during the lockdowns of Covid 19 people were encouraged to get on zoom and do videos just to be seen. Yet, as I discovered that day, dark places produce the most wonderful creations of our Father God.

What an encouragement for each of us, the world is a very dark place. Be encouraged, God is creating growth, beautiful growth behind all that darkness, and one day it will be revealed for everyone to see.

Prayer:

God, please strengthen our faith to know that your work is still being done even in the darkest places of our world. If we rest in you and stay where you have planted us, you will do a great thing and it will be something astonishing. Amen.

He Knows My Name

One evening I was listening to an ewe and lamb calling each other across the paddock next to the house. It amazes me how each mother knows which lamb is hers. In a mob of sheep, I have often wondered why any lamb wouldn't just get a feed from the nearest ewe that has food to provide. Yet, this doesn't happen, very rarely will another ewe mother a lamb that isn't hers.

As I listened, I remembered how, if I was in a crowded supermarket I could always tell where my children were, my hearing always seemed to be able to hone in on them. It's a very special gift that God endowed mothers with, mothers of a lot of species, particularly those who carry offspring inside of them.

What was more astonishing to me, is that God, who created me, has that same ability to hear my voice in amongst the noise of the world around me. There is so much going on around the world, wars, crime, apathy, and anger just to name a few, that can distract us and thwart our ability to hear those things that we should be focused on, yet God doesn't get distracted, each time we call out to Him, He hears us, He knows exactly what we are saying and how we are feeling and He is ready to answer us, maybe not at that moment, but when the time is right.

"I am the good shepherd. I know my own, and I'm known by my own;" (John 10:14)

If you think about each person that has been created, He hears them, each and every time they cry out to Him, whether it is on a regular basis, or a first-time cry for help.

"For, "Whoever will call on the name of the Lord will be saved." (Romans 10:13)

It's great to remember that the God who created you, knows your voice, which is just so special to Him and He will always hear you, regardless of how many times you call on His name.

Hell

Scrolling through my social media while away on a break with my daughter, I discovered that another fire had broken out near my home. That, coupled with the constant reminders of other parts of Australia burning on the TV, made my heart sink with a cry of 'when will this ever end'.

The following conversation happened as a result.
'Can you imagine what hell will be like?'
'Much the same as Australia right now.'

'Yes, but can you envisage that in hell it is going to go on for ever and ever, with no end in sight?'

There have been many reports of miracles that allowed some people to experience the extraordinary grace of God and filling them with hope for the future. At least we know that this season will end eventually, but once we cross the barrier between here and there, there is no hope, no end in sight ever. The grace that we saw extended during those fires will no longer be available.

This is what our Lord came to save us from. Not the fires here and now but the eternal ones that will go on for eternity.

Aussie's often joke about hell being like the pub with no beer, well sorry everyone, it's not. It's like being in the middle of a fire storm.

"So shall it be at the end of the world: the angels shall come forth, and sever the wicked from among the just, And shall cast them into the furnace of fire: there shall be wailing and gnashing of teeth". Matthew 30:49-50.

For those who have already lost loved ones, hope still exists as no one knows what goes on in the last moments of their lives. God doesn't want anyone to live eternity in hell so I'm sure that He makes every effort to reach out to all those in their last moments.

"Jesus saith unto him, I am the way, the truth, and the life: no man cometh unto the Father, but by me." John 14:6.

Prayer:

Lord, may the knowledge of what could await us in the future allow us to make the right decision in the here and now. We thank you with grateful hearts for the grace you have shown us in this time of crisis. Please Lord, take mercy on our land soon and send fire quenching and drought breaking rain to renew our land. Forgive us for all the times that we have ignored your grace in the past and may we all continue to praise you while we have breath to do so.

Home

Since the children have left home, I have found myself travelling around the property more and more with my husband. It was something that I didn't do much of while I was caught up with home duties and employment. I just didn't have the time. What I have learnt though, is that there are few places where the house and sheds cannot be seen. The roof and buildings are light in colour, so it makes it much easier to see them. Sure, there are some places where they are hidden from sight, but they seem far and few between.

It's nice to know that, with the house being so visible, it wouldn't be hard to find my way back home if we ever broke down and had to walk back. My sense of direction is pretty bad, and if I didn't have the visual landmark to aim for, I could end up anywhere.

I thought about how God is just as visible to all of us, no matter where we are. His light will always be there to show us where home is, and if we stray away from Him, we only have to take one step to be back in the arms of Jesus.

There was another thought that occurred to me and that is that no matter where I was on the farm I was still home, it just wasn't as comfortable as it would be in the house.

We all have times when life throws us into the midst of a storm. These may not necessarily be of our making, just like Job's situation when the devil tried to get him to curse God by taking away all the blessings that God had given him.

Like Job, there will be times when life is uncomfortable, but we are still safely in God's vision and wrapped up in His presence and we can thank Him every day for watching over us.

John 6:37 says, "All those whom the Father gives me will come to me. He who comes to me I will in no way throw out."

Remember, no matter what we are facing, God is just a prayer away.

How Embarrassing

The faithful believers in Australia bowed their heads in prayer for a month, they desperately wanted the drought to break. Another month passed and there was still no sign of the drought-breaking rain that was so badly needed. Does this mean that God hadn't answered our prayers? Of course not! It seems that the answer was that we needed to wait a little longer.

There has been some very good rain in some places that have suffered from devasting bushfires. However, as I read posts of thanks, I'm constantly embarrassed. Reading the posts, thinking this is wonderful for these people, and then getting to the end and there is invariably a final sentence that says: Keep sending it down.... Followed by names such as Hughie, and I even saw a new one, Marg. Oh, why do people have to spoil such a good gift with such a sarcastic remark?

Exodus 20:7 says: "You shall not take the name of the LORD your God in vain, for the LORD will not hold *him* guiltless who takes His name in vain." Yes, we are used to applying this commandment to those who use the name of Jesus as a swear word. Even young children get this. One young student accused a scripture teacher of saying a bad word, when she told the class that she was there to teach them about God and Jesus. Such was their understanding of our Lord.

However, do we realise that when we call God by any other name other than His real title, we are also taking His name in vain?

"For thou shalt worship no other god: for the LORD, whose name *is* Jealous, *is* a jealous God:" Exodus 34:14.

There have been times when people have called me by a name other than the name I prefer and I have been quick to correct them, sometimes politely, and other times with less grace. We have heard the joke: You can call me anything as long as you don't call me late for dinner, this is used by many people to reduce the embarrassment of someone for forgetting their name.

How can we forget the name of God? What becomes so obvious, is just how patient and loving our God is. He is so gracious. If it was me, I know that I would be holding back the rain for longer, or striking people with lightning, but God continues to endow these people with the much-needed rain.

"And the LORD passed by before him, and proclaimed, The LORD, The LORD God, merciful and gracious, longsuffering, and abundant in goodness and truth," Exodus 34:6.

Prayer:

Lord, we thank you for your patience and love. Please forgive us for all the times that your name has been taken in vain and may you continue to send us the much-needed rain. Lord, we know that, one day, your name will be glorified because when you act there will be no doubt that you have worked amongst your people.

I'm doomed.

The tears ran down my face. My brain had locked onto a conspiracy theory. This Covid 19 virus was made to just get rid of the old people in our society. If it worked, imagine how much money governments around the world would save. While I'm not considered old yet, I am headed in that direction, fast. There just didn't seem to be the respect for older people that there used to be, in fact, respect for human life seems to have gone by the wayside. A heavy feeling of doom came over me.

Through the tears, God whispered one name, over, and over again: Moses.

As the tears dried, I remembered that his generation lived through another virus, called Pharaoh. It (He) struck every Israelite male as they were born and yet, Moses was saved.

Then there was the Herod virus that killed the children of Bethlehem who were under two years of age. On this occasion, I imagine that many children who were born in that two-year period might have been saved simply because their parents had returned to their second homes, from which they had travelled for the census and Jesus, who Herod was after, had escaped because of Joseph's wisdom in listening to God.

The reality is, that all through history, there have been times when evil has disrespected human life and tried its hardest to do away with it on a mass scale.

Yet, above all, there have also been those who have, one way or another, survived against impossible odds, or to put it correctly, God has covered and protected for His own purpose.

Are we privy to that purpose? Not always. Can we understand why He protected some and not others? Not likely.

"For who hath known the mind of the Lord? or who hath been his counsellor?" Romans 11:34.

But, through it all, we need to trust that He will bring an end to the evil sooner rather than later because in the bigger plan, He wants His creation to endure.

"And we know that all things work together for good to them that love God, to them who are the called according to his purpose." Romans 8:28.

Prayer:

Lord, forgive us for all the times we have not respected your human creation. Thank you for reminding all of us, that above all, you will limit what evil can do. Your purpose is greater than any evil that man can create. We pray for those who are grieving because of the effects of this current virus, whatever they might look like, give them comfort and strength and may they look forward in faith to a time when this too, will pass.

I'm going away.

The excitement bubbled up inside me! The border bubble had been extended and I would finally be able to visit my family in Queensland. Having been in lockdown for so long without any cases of Covid-19 in our area for months, meant that, like many people, I was frustrated at being locked up for what seemed to be no good reason.

As I planned, and yes, danced around the house, God asked me another question. Why don't you get this excited about seeing me or going to Heaven?

It's a good question, one, to my shame, that I don't have an answer to yet.

Is it because it's an unknown destination for many of us?

Is it because most of us know that in order to get there we have to go through a very dark place, that is, the process of dying? That process can be very difficult and painful. Would we be more excited if we knew that we would, one night, just fall asleep and wake up on the other side?

Or is it simply that we are still too rooted in the here and now?

Maybe you are one of those people who get up in the morning and dance around saying that if today was the day that you went home to Jesus, it would be the greatest thing to happen.

Colossians 3:1-7 says "Since, then, you have been raised with Christ, set your hearts on things above, where Christ is, seated at the right hand of God. Set your minds on things above, not on earthly things. For you died, and your life is now hidden with Christ in God. When Christ, who is your life, appears, then you also will appear with him in glory. Put to death, therefore, whatever belongs to your earthly nature: sexual immorality, impurity, lust, evil desires, and greed, which is idolatry. Because of these, the wrath of God is coming. You used to walk in these ways, in the life you once lived."

I am constantly reminded that I also have to live in a world that needs to hear that there is a Heaven to go to and maybe that would be easier if I was more excited about going there myself.

Paul said in Philippians 1:22 "For to me to live *is* Christ, and to die *is* gain. But if I live in the flesh, this *is* the fruit of my labour: yet what I shall choose I wot not." Which tells me that he also felt the tension between working for the Lord here and looking forward to Heaven.

I guess this is a tension that we all feel while living here?

It's not over yet!

The drought started to break, and people were starting to say things like, you are alright now. It was as if one good fall of rain was going to make everything better. It had happened before and so I wrote the following letter. Romans 12:12 says; rejoicing in hope, patient in tribulation, continuing steadfastly in prayer; I wanted everyone to know that we were still doing all three.

To our City Brothers and Sisters.

While some of us have received rain and it finally looks like we might be able to move forward and sow crops and find grass for our stock, I am very conscious that many haven't received any rain yet, and if the rains don't keep coming, we are going be in trouble for a lot longer.

However, if the rains continue and the drought breaks, I'd like you all to be aware that our farming families will be doing it tough for a number of years yet. Here is one case study for you.

A neighbour sold his barley crop before the drought at the record price of $400 per tonne. When he made inquiries the other day to buy seed to sow again, he was informed that the price was now $1600 per tonne. We priced other seeds, and their prices are higher than that again. Anyone that kept seed back for replanting will have had to use that to keep their stock alive, or sold it to buy hay, groceries, and pay bills, and you can be guaranteed that if those crops are successful the price will drop considerably. The best-case scenario is that we may break even, not make money. If rains don't keep coming, then ….

Please also be aware that even if, and that's a big IF, the drought is over, your country brothers and sisters are going to need your support for many years to come. If they have stock, any increase in their numbers are going to have to be held onto, not sold, in order to build their stock numbers. We went from 1200 sheep to less than 300 and there are no lambs yet. A sheep has to carry a lamb for around 5 months before its born and a cow over nine months. It then has to be grown out to a certain weight before a farmer can even consider selling it. Calves take even longer. We have seen it happen before where people, particularly politicians, think that once it rains, farmers are back on their feet and rolling in money. Rolling in green grass is very different to rolling in the 'green stuff'.

Please remember, rain only brings hope, it doesn't rain dollars and cents.

Job

Maybe it's a birthday, a new year, or some anniversary where you take time to reflect on the year that has gone and the year ahead. As you look forward, are you seeing challenges, problems, and dramas that are making you think that this year isn't going to be any better than the previous one. I was thinking about Job, and while the Bible doesn't give us a particular time, I can imagine Satan having the conversation with God at the end of the year, as it's a time for everyone to reflect on what was and what might be ahead of them.

Let's, for one-minute, place the story of Job during the early stages of a new year. We know that there was a celebration at his eldest son's house presumably for his birthday, which would have caused some refection on what the last year had been and what the new year for him might bring. The positivity that he felt as his family reflected and said goodbye to the old year and looked forward to a new and even more prosperous year, was shattered in a matter of a few days.

That's a lot of grief to carry on with!

Yet, he continued to worship God.

"Then Job arose, and tore his robe, and shaved his head, and fell down on the ground, and worshiped. He said, "Naked I came out of my mother's womb, and naked will I return there. Yahweh gave, and Yahweh has taken away. Blessed be Yahweh's name."

In all this, Job didn't sin, nor charge God with wrongdoing." (Job 1:20-22).

Let's not forget that, just like us, Job had to deal with the emotional consequences of this time for the rest of his life, no number of children could replace those that he'd lost, no amount of wealth would bring them back to him, but God faithfully saw him through and He will continue to see you through whatever last year, and this year, will give you.

No matter how crazy your world becomes, will you remember that God is in control, he has set a hedge around you and, therefore, continue to say with Job: "But as for me, I know that my Redeemer lives." Job 19:25.

Kill it with Love.

We have a particular grass that isn't native to Australia but flourishes at the expense of the native and improved pastures that are needed to help our stock to grow and thrive. Even if you cut it down and leave it lying on the ground it releases a chemical that kills anything underneath it.

The advice we were given to try and get rid of this invasive pest was to shower it with love. That is: we should pour lots and lots of fertilizer on it, that grass cannot take fertility. This would not only improve the soil, but the grass would grow so fast that it would not cope and, therefore, die.

How does this relate to us as Christians? We are dealing with a trend in our culture that is draining the life out of our society. I suspect that the best way to stop it spreading is to kill it with love. The love that God gives, and which should flow through us and out into the world around us.

Mathew 5:43-48: "You have heard that it was said, 'Love your neighbour and hate your enemy.' But I tell you, love your enemies and pray for those who persecute you, that you may be children of your Father in heaven. He causes his sun to rise on the evil and the good, and sends rain on the righteous and the unrighteous. If you love those who love you, what reward will you get? Are not even the tax collectors doing that? And if you greet only your own people, what are you doing more than others? Do not even pagans do that? Be perfect, therefore, as your heavenly Father is perfect."

No, this is not an easy task, but we have the greatest power at our disposal. Let's ask God to give us the strength, courage, and motivation to not just tell people that Jesus is the answer to their problems but also show them how much He loves them. James chapter two helps us to know the wisdom of this.

Prayer:

Father, we come to you asking for strength, courage, and the filling of the Holy Spirit in order to carry out the work that you have given us to do in this time where people are so lost and confused. Help us to show, more than tell, the world that you love them and desire to have a new relationship with them that will enable them to live eternally in Heaven with you once their time on this earth is over.

Learning God's Way

One thing I have learnt about how God teaches us, is that He takes us forward one step at a time. I have seen this not only in the business that we have started recently but throughout my life. As I look back, I see that many learning experiences were warm-up exercises for events that I couldn't see in my future. When our children go to school, we don't expect them to go backwards in their learning skills when they move up at the beginning of each year. God doesn't expect us to do this either.

2020 was tough for most of us and we prayed that 2021 will be better and less stressful.

But... there was a lot of internet chatter about war and persecution coming to Australia. So, what if this is just a prelude to something tougher. Has this year just been our warm-up exercises for tougher times ahead?

There are two examples in the Bible of places that were facing destruction because of their unfaithfulness to God. Sodom & Gomorrah, and Nineveh, one was destroyed and the other saved. Are the visions seen by so many about the destruction of Australia, set in stone, maybe or maybe not.

One thing is certain, that no matter what is ahead of us as a nation, or even the world, God has a job for each of us, that of showing His love to everyone we come in contact with, praying for those who are against us and becoming closer to the Lord as He helps us to navigate whatever happens. Yes, we might hope that the future will be easier but if it isn't, we will be stronger for it.

"Consider it pure joy, my brothers and sisters, whenever you face trials of many kinds, because you know that the testing of your faith produces perseverance. Let perseverance finish its work so that you may be mature and complete, not lacking anything." James 1:2-4.

Is Less More?

Some people have suggested that Covid was a way for God to send us to our room to think about our value systems. If this was the case: what good things could come with this brave new world that will be our new normal?

"Be still, and know that I *am* God: I will be exalted among the heathen, I will be exalted in the earth." Psalm 46:10.

The internet has become our shopping centre. If we want to sell, then I suggest that those who are honest, reliable, and market wisely are going to be able to survive longer than those who market for a quick buck. However, we also have learnt that computers and the internet are not replacements for everything, particularly the face-to-face teaching of our children.

Putting all our eggs in one basket has taught us that, when the basket gets smashed, so do most of the eggs, so in our brave new world, we need to find more baskets to work with. Yes, this is going to mean that we have to get fitter, mentally, physically, and emotionally.

Planning for functions has become way more complicated these days as we learn in a post Covid world. There is going to have to be a return to the old way of sending invitations and RSVPs. Something that we have lost in the pre-Covid world.

We could, if we are willing, realise that people are more important than the dollar and goods. The neighbour next door needs to be visited and made to feel valued.

"This is my commandment, That ye love one another, as I have loved you." John 15:12.

In the new world, the job market, while different, is still going to be smaller, I fear, and so those that have jobs will need to be diligent, and those that don't have work, may find that any job is better than no job at all. I also think that wages will need to flatten. This of course, may not happen.

"Better *is* little with the fear of the LORD than great treasure and trouble therewith." Proverbs 15:16

I know this sounds so late 1940's, early 1950's, but then here's the thing: we had a much better quality of life, as opposed to quantity of stuff.

As we look, not to the things that are seen, but to the things that are unseen. For the things that are seen are transient, but the things that are unseen are eternal. 2 Corinthians 4:18.

Surely, we will, in this brave new world, realise that less is more.

Life can be a Puzzle.

I have a computer game, called Ball Sort, that I sometimes play. The point of it, is to shift the different lines of coloured dots, or balls, which are all mixed up, around so that you end up with the same-coloured balls in one line. You only have two spare lines to work with.

There are some days when a game seems to be effortless, and I can manage success without a lot of trouble. However, there are some games which I have to start over, time and again and even put it down for a while before I can manage to solve it. Some puzzles just don't make sense until later.

I noticed one morning that the puzzle was much closer to real life than I was previously willing to give it credit for. I'm sure that we have all had situations where things didn't make sense and it didn't matter how many solutions you manage to come up with, nothing worked.

Like the time we opened a shop. We had been looking at different premises for a couple of years and nothing seemed to be suitable. When the one we really liked came available, the owner decided that he wanted more money than he had initially indicated, which was okay, because we realised that there would be insufficient power outlets for our computers anyway. Eventually, a very small shop front came up in a completely different location and we opened. A couple of weeks later another shop owner in the same street came to visit and regaled us with all the advantages of being in that particular position as opposed to the other one. Finally, what God had chosen for us made much more sense and we were able to learn a great deal while we worked out of that place including what we really needed when we have to move.

That's what makes the Ball Sort Puzzle so similar to life. Those balls don't move by themselves, someone has to shift them and decide where they should be put. Just as in our lives, God doesn't always move things for us remotely, he has given us brains, imagination, voices, hands, and feet and He expects us to put them to good use in order to solve our problems. He will not do for us what we can do for ourselves.

There will be times when life doesn't make sense and no matter what we try, nothing seems to work, but if we keep going, keep praying, and keep trying, then one day, things will fall into place and things will make sense.

Galatians 6:9 says: "Let's not be weary in doing good, for we will reap in due season if we don't give up."

Limiting God

Do we limit God, try to put Him in a box without even realising it? I do sometimes.

I walked through the kitchen and stopped at the family room arch, there on the TV was the news that Notre Dame Cathedral was burning. As I looked at the news, what struck me was that the reporters were saying that it had been burning for over six hours while I was tucked up safely in bed and totally unaware that this great tragedy was underway. This has happened more than once, those of us in the southern hemisphere wake to find that some event of great significance has taken place on the other side of the world while we slept.

When we talk about the return of Jesus, so many people cite the fact that the existence of the internet and international news service would facilitate the whole world being able to see the return of Christ at the same time. I've never really been convinced, even as a teenager. However, there were times when everyone in the family was having trouble sleeping, that I did wonder if, on the night Jesus returns, no one would be able to sleep. The older I get the less I'm convinced about both these.

"And he shall send his angels with a great sound of a trumpet, and they shall gather together his elect from the four winds, from one end of heaven to the other." Matthew 24:31 tells us that Jesus' return will not be silent, unlike His first arrival. There will be so much noise that I'm sure everyone will be woken and will be rushing outside in order to see what is going on. It won't matter which part of the world we live in, or what time of day it will be. We will all see with our own eyes such a massive event.

The suggestion that technology is going to be used to help us view this event is, in my mind, a means of limiting God. To me, it's a lack of faith that God is greater than anything He allows us to invent.

Sadly, as I pondered this, I realised that I was doing the same thing to God in my everyday life. I limit God by not having enough faith that He can work outside the parameters of my daily life. I expected God to act in accordance with my limited expectations and experiences.

"For my thoughts *are* not your thoughts, neither *are* your ways my ways, saith the LORD." Isaiah 55:8.

Lord, please forgive my unbelief.

Do you find yourself doubting that God will work outside the boxes that we put Him in?

Little Things

I was listening to the story of John Newton and the tough start he had to life. I couldn't help but think about how his life was similar to Paul's, not that we know much about Paul's early life. However, both these men had persecuted Jesus, and both had been saved by the grace of God.

"And as he journeyed, he came near Damascus: and suddenly there shined round about him a light from heaven: And he fell to the earth, and heard a voice saying unto him, Saul, Saul, why persecutest thou me?" Acts 9:3-4.

"And the King shall answer and say unto them, Verily I say unto you, Inasmuch as ye have done *it* unto one of the least of these my brethren, ye have done *it* unto me." Matthew 24:40.

It's wonderful how God can turn the lives of those who repent of their sin around and make them instruments to spread His word around the world, long after they have gone home to be with their Lord.

There are many more stories that can be found about how faithful servants, even in the small things, have had an impact on this world long after they have passed onto the next. Every person who has been considered to be a powerful force for the Lord were led to the Lord by someone who was faithful in teaching His word. They may have been a Sunday school teacher, a father, a mother, a preacher, or a neighbour.

It doesn't matter who we are, if we are faithful in telling others about the love of God, in whatever way we are comfortable with, God will use those efforts long after we have gone to Heaven, and we may not even be aware of our impact until the day we stand before Him on Judgement Day.

Prayer:

Thank you for being able to use all our efforts no matter how small they are.

Living like Gideon

Judges 6:1-4

Let's take a closer look at this passage from Judges. What struck me about this story was how close it is to the current situation in Australia.

Verse 1 says: "The Israelites did evil in the eyes of the Lord, and for seven years he gave them into the hands of the Midianites."

Very few of us would argue that we, as a country, have done evil in the eyes of God. You only have to watch the daily news reports to know that indictment also applies to the 21st century Australia and that doesn't take in the laws that are being passed by our lawmakers.

So, who are our Midianites? Those who oppress us. Well, you can probably take your pick here. For those on the land, there are a number of forces at work tyrannizing them. Those who do not agree with their way of life, and those who falsely accuse them of decimating our land come to mind immediately. As the Midianites were actual invaders then you could even add the increase in wildlife and feral creatures to the list. In many places in Australia the rapid increase in wild dogs and pigs have made it impossible for farmers to make a living out of their traditional systems.

Verse 2: "Because the power of Midian was so oppressive, the Israelites prepared shelters for themselves in mountain clefts, caves and strongholds."

Many farmers now find that they have to surround their places with exclusion fencing to protect their livestock and crops. Sure, you may not agree that they are on par with shelters in mountain clefts or caves, but they are a very necessary and expensive outlay if they are to, not only protect their animals and crops, but allow them to feed their families.

Verses 3 & 4: "Whenever the Israelites planted their crops, the Midianites, Amalekites, and other eastern people invaded the country. They camped on the land and ruined the crops all the way to Gaza and did not spare a living thing for Israel, neither sheep nor cattle nor donkeys." "Their livestock and their tents like swarms of locusts". Here again, the imagination doesn't have to move very far to realise that drought and rural crime carry out the same devastation that these foreign powers inflicted on Gideon and his fellow countrymen.

Yet, the farmers keep going, just as Gideon continued to find different ways to provide for his family. They know that God is in control and one day He will bring justice.

Looking Forward or Back

The year is coming to a close. Are you looking back and thinking about how you might have done some things differently? When we look back at what we have done, often we lament things that we haven't managed to do, but we can also rejoice in things that we have achieved. It's a natural process that happens towards the end of events, we assess which things worked and those that didn't. As we age, some of us look back and say that if we had our time over again, we would do some things differently and some things we wouldn't.

In Matthew 25:14-30 we read about three servants, all of whom are given talents equal to their skill sets. They are given the job of making the most of what they have been given. Two servants succeed, the third one doesn't. Interestingly, it's the servant with the least who fails. As humans we often expect the one with the most, the one who will most likely take the biggest risks, to be the one who will fail. Yet, here both the servants with more succeeded.

I thought about the third servant. Was he afraid, not only of his master, but of failing? I also wondered if that inner voice in his head kept telling him that because he had only been given one talent that he was already a failure, he didn't have the right skills to turn a profit. Maybe that voice told him that if he had the right skills, he would have been given more and, therefore, he was domed before he had begun. Did this feed his fear to the point that all he could manage was to dig a hole and put his talent in it? I imagine him looking over his shoulder the whole time, hoping no one saw where he had put it, fearing that it might even be stolen. After the Master had his say and took things off him, I'm certain that this young man was definitely one person who looked back and said, 'I wish I had done things differently'.

As I read this story, I thought of a lady I once knew, Eva. The thing that impressed me the most about her, was that no matter how badly her hands hurt (she suffered from chronic arthritis) or how much pain she was in, she insisted on getting her own cup of tea. Nearly every time I offered to get it for her, her response was, if I don't use it, I'll lose it. Her skill set had been diminished, radically, yet she persisted in working with what she had.

So, how did your year go? Are there things that you would do differently? I'm sure there are, even if they are only small things. I shouldn't have grumbled so much, smiled more, talked less, stood my ground more, maybe even been a little more generous. This list might be endless.

However, coming to the end of something also means that we are approaching something new. The end of any year means that there is a new year just around the corner. When we finish working in a certain field, we often start a new career, even if it's called retirement, and when we reach the end of our earthly life, we are about to begin our new eternal one.

So, let's approach our new year with the small resources that we have; our aching bones and health issues, our lack of funds, and very little time. If you cannot do anything else, you can pray. Let's not bury our talents with excuses and fear but look at ways we can serve Him by working with what we have and look to our Master who loves us with great patience.

"And let us not be weary in well doing: for in due season we shall reap, if we faint not." Galatians 6:9.

What are you planning to do for God next year?

Lost

I was surprised, one morning, to discover a Pelican in our backyard. He seemed very quiet, hanging around for three days, even trying to make friends with our Guinea fowls that roamed freely.

After the first day of wandering around the yard, he decided that our verandah, in front of our door, was a very nice place to sit. He sat there for hours just watching what we're doing.

This guy was well and truly out of his proper environment, after all we live more than four hours by car from the sea and we began to be concerned that without water, even fresh water, he would end up dying. There wasn't even a fishpond in our backyard, and he just didn't seem inclined to try and move on.

After three days, my husband was concerned enough to try and force him towards a large dam on our property. As the story goes, the bird, under protest, moved down the paddock until he saw the water, and then he knew where he wanted to go, and the protests stopped.

Sometimes, we can be like our pelican friend. We lose our way, it's easier than we think, sometimes, for no reason that we can put our finger on, we find ourselves somewhere that is unfamiliar and, in some way, most likely dangerous. It doesn't even matter how we got there, what is important is that God knows where He wants us and exactly where that place is. So, He starts to move us forward, and yes, like our pelican, we protest and grumble, however eventually, most often in hindsight, we find that God has pushed us to the very best place for us.

Romans 8:28 says, "And we know that all things work together for good to them that love God, to them who are the called according to *his* purpose."

Sometimes it's hard to understand where God is taking us but let us remember that He sees more than we can ever see, and He only wants the best for us.

Making the Bed

I've only just managed to get into the habit of making the beds in our house as early in the morning as it possible. Each time I walk past a bedroom and see the bed made, I relax a bit more, but I also hear my mother's voice in my head telling me for years how, if the bed is made, it makes it look as if a lot of your housework is done and I wonder why it took me so long to get into this habit? Why didn't I insist that the children learn to make their beds as they got out of them?

It's hard to say, but when the children were little, like most mothers, I hit the floor running, getting my husband's lunch ready, children out of bed and ready for school, getting myself ready for work, making sure that the washing was done, dishes washed, attending to the thousands of questions that were fired at me, particularly while I was in the middle of something else, and attending to whatever emergency that always seemed to happen at a most inconvenient moment.

When there was a quiet moment, and it usually was just a moment, all I wanted to do was sit and be myself. The bed making was one of the last things on my list.

So, what is God trying to teach me each time I pass that bedroom? Maybe, that there is no point beating myself up over what I didn't do or what I should have done. I have to forget the past, move on, after all I cannot change what is behind me, I can only look forward with renewed optimism now that I have started, I can continue in His strength.

"Brothers, I don't regard myself as yet having taken hold, but one thing I do: forgetting the things which are behind and stretching forward to the things which are before," Philippians 3:13.

Messy Tangles

"Every wise woman builds her house, but the foolish one tears it down with her own hands." Proverbs 14:1.

Does the house you are building go smoothly or does it get into messy tangles?

One year, I decided to make things for my family instead of buying Christmas gifts. The idea came when, earlier in the year, one grandson asked for a knitted jumper, with hood and diagonal stripes. If I did it for one, I should do it for all my grandchildren. I'm wise enough to know that it's important to treat all the children equally.

I was about to relish the blessing of only a few grandchildren.

I found a pattern, a friend helped me learn some of the skills needed, purchased yarn, and plunged in. I'm no professional and the yarn got tangled. I found a major mistake, pulled it undone, and started again. This happened three more times until I finally managed to make progress. However, it didn't matter how hard I tried, the yarn constantly got into a tangle, not small ones but big messy knots. Sometimes I was able to keep working by just pulling the yarn through the mess, but eventually I would have to stop and unravel the mess before I could move on.

The other projects were pretty straight forward, but there were times when I thought I was silly to even start this project. I started without the proper skill set to complete it smoothly. Some days I had to be very determined to pick it up and continue. However, I pushed on and it was completed several weeks before Christmas and there was one very happy grandson when he opened his gift. I feel sure that it strengthened the connection between us.

Build your house!

Like knitting that jumper, in the process of building our families, (house) we often get into real tangles. We make mistakes, fall down, get up, pull the threads of our lives out of the mess, start again, and reknit them back together.

Don't give up building your home with determination and patience, no matter how many times you fall down; start again! Remember God is always there to give you the wisdom you need.

James 1:5 says: "But if any of you lacks wisdom, let him ask of God, who gives to all liberally and without reproach, and it will be given to him."

Mother's Day

Matthew 12:46-50

In Australia, April and May sees the celebration of Mother's Day as a significant financial focus for our stores. However, it can be an emotional one for many of us. That emotional focus can be one of almost frantic activity; making sure that the house is cleaned and ready for our little people to stay safe when they come to visit, or it might be one of relaxed anticipation, knowing that the family will be giving us a break from our normal duties. However, I suspect that for many of us it is more likely to be one of sadness, if not trepidation, because we are aware that our mothering skills are not appreciated and we no longer have our own mothers to share our feelings with.

Yet, in the Bible passage, Jesus tells us that the church is our family. Each of us has a mother, a son, a daughter that we are required to care for and be cared for, even though we haven't got a birth connection to them; they are part of His family and, therefore, part of ours.

The challenge is for each one of us to relate to each member of His family. It can be difficult to know what is the best way to make those connections. Not just on Mother's Day, but every day. Let's be mindful and ask Him to show us, those who are sailing through troubled waters, who might be sinking in a sea of loneliness, drowning under financial pressure, or just being rocked about by the waves of demands in their daily duties. Let's ask God to help us connect with them in a meaningful way that will help them to feel as if they really are part of God's family which is the Church.

Prayer:

God, you have given us each a very special family to be part of. We thank you for the privilege and we ask for your grace to be the best that we can be as we interact with each other.

Moving

There had been a lot of moving in our family circle during a particular year. One child has moved from the city to the country, to temporary accommodation, and then to a more permanent space. In amongst all this moving we had also moved into a temporary shop front and then found that we were looking for a new premises to carry on our work. Needless to say, there were several times when it was stated, I just want to stay put for a while.

Constant moving can be very unsettling, physically and emotionally, but thinking about this one morning, I realized some things about our lives here on earth. If we don't keep moving, we never move forward, isn't there a saying that says; if you don't use it, you lose it? Yes, that saying is usually related to body functions, such as moving a leg, using our brain, or the like, if we don't, often they will cease up and become very stiff or stop working.

Our lives involve moving in the form of growth, we move from one stage of life to another, and if we didn't, we would stop growing.

The most important thing that I remembered was that we are really only travelling through our lives here, we are on our way to our eternal destination, which ever one that might be. Even those who have no faith understand that life here is only temporary. The Bible tells us that we should set our eyes on the heavenly destination. Isaiah 43:18 says: "Don't remember the former things, and don't consider the things of old. Behold, I will do a new thing. It springs out now. Don't you know it? I will even make a way in the wilderness, and rivers in the desert."

Keeping our focus on our Heavenly destination, helps us to stay anchored to the one thing that will never change, our God who never changes and Heaven which will always be perfect forever and ever.

Musical Masterpiece

I woke up one morning, just as dawn was breaking, to the sound of a bird singing. It's a pretty sound and I always enjoy listening to it. It wasn't long though before a few more birds joined in, with their different voices. It got me wondering how someone would be able to capture that sounds and turn them into a musical score for a band or an orchestra. It would take someone with a great deal of talent and a lot of skill to turn it into a musical masterpiece.

As I listened, I realized that they were all allowed to sing freely. If they weren't there would have been a different tone to the notes, there was no squabbling just happy bird noises. Yes, there were times when one bird dominated the rest, but they didn't seem to mind, even if it didn't sound quite so great to me, they just let them sing their hearts out.

Our lives are often very much like that musical chorus that played that morning, there are a lot of different songs that we have to play. On any given day we have to respond as siblings, children of aging parents, parents to our own, work colleagues, friends, home owners, and the list goes on. Some of these things enter our lives uninvited, and some we allow in for various reasons, and yet we still have to make it all mesh together so we don't end up in a screaming heap and most of us can't do it alone.

There is someone who can take charge of our lives and direct us, just as a conductor directs an orchestra and that person is God.

He knows what we are capable of, what needs to dominate at what time and how to make everything work together to make our own particular, beautiful, musical masterpiece.

"Man's goings *are* of the LORD; how can a man then understand his own way?" Proverbs 20:24.

"And we know that all things work together for good to them that love God, to them who are the called according to *his* purpose." Romans 8:28.

I know that sometimes our lives seem to have no rhythm or reason to it but be reassured that God is the master director and He knows exactly how things will be worked out.

New Shoes

While in lockdown, during the world Corvid 19 pandemic, as winter approached, I found my feet were in my slippers more than shoes. I found myself wanting to buy a new pair of shoes for no other reason, than to glue my slippers to the heels to give myself the height that slippers don't.

While I was thinking about new shoes, and how uncomfortable they can be to start with, I remembered that Queen Elizabeth had a staff member who wore her new shoes for a period of time before she had to wear them in order to 'break them in' so they wouldn't hurt the Queen's feet during formal engagements.

At the same time, I was thinking about the different stages of life, how just like new shoes, feeling a little uncomfortable as we learn new strategies, skills, and get stretched emotionally for a while is common. We just master one stage, when we find ourselves in another new one and we have to start all over again.

Most stories, from the fairy tales we read as children, to the novels read as adults generally end with a version of 'and they lived happily ever after'. We are conditioned to believe that in real life we should get to a certain point in life and 'happy ever after' kicks in. Life stops being a struggle and find that when it doesn't come, we should try to make it happen.

Our happily ever after will come, if, while we are here on earth, we have a relationship with Jesus. He helps us navigate the tough times here and will make sure of our entry to Heaven.

"But now they desire a better *country*, that is, an heavenly: wherefore God is not ashamed to be called their God: for he hath prepared for them a city." Hebrews 11:16.

Life will always be a little uncomfortable here on earth, but our happy ever after awaits us in Heaven.

New Year Resolutions

Did you make a list of New Year Resolutions? There is usually a lot of discussion about them at that time of the year. There was one year, in the middle of the pandemic, (2020/2021) when there was very little discussion about resolutions. This was most likely a result of people realizing that plans (resolutions), can be derailed in an instant on a major scale.

Most of us already knew that this was possible on a personal level but there are many mentors who shout that plans could come to fruition if you work hard enough, believe in yourself, and be positive enough about the outcomes; you are the only limiting factor.

The pandemic taught us the reality of what James wrote many years ago: "Whereas you don't know what your life will be like tomorrow. For what is your life? For you are a vapor that appears for a little time, and then vanishes away. For you ought to say, "If the Lord wills, we will both live, and do this or that." James 4:14-15.

However, so many people found that this forced change of direction was a good thing, they were able to reevaluate their value systems and what is really important to them. Yes, the process was painful and difficult, but what good things in life aren't?

If your plans for this year are already going astray because of things outside your control, remember that there may be a good reason why God has allowed this to happen. He loves you and wants the very best for you. So, look to God and ask Him where He wants you to go, stand tall, take His hand, and let Him lead you forward without looking back and remember what David learnt.

"The steps of a *good* man are ordered by the LORD: and he delighteth in his way. Though he fall, he shall not be utterly cast down: for the LORD upholdeth *him with* his hand." Psalm 37:23-24. And Solomon says in Proverbs 16:9 "A man's heart deviseth his way: but the LORD directeth his steps."

Making plans is a good thing, as long as we leave room for God to take us in a different direction if He wants us to do something different.

Nothing New

While babysitting my granddaughter, I watched her playing with an empty box. I smiled and thought, children don't change. Give them something inexpensive and they play quite happily. It's hard to imagine our life without this little body. She makes such a wonderful contribution to our lives, tantrums and all.

A couple of days later, I was thinking about the abortion bill being presented to the New South Wales Parliament. It occurred to me that maybe society hasn't changed much either. "The thing that hath been, it *is that* which shall be; and that which is done *is* that which shall be done: and *there is* no new *thing* under the sun." Ecclesiastes 1:9.

It seems to me that we haven't moved on from the days when two women stood before Solomon asking for his judgement. One wanting to care for a baby and the other wanted to use it for reasons of her own. 1 Kings 3:16-28. Now, there are just many more women and many more babies. Some wanting to care and nurture children but unable to for whatever reason, others being able to but not wanting to.

While I understand that many people would consider this issue far more complicated than it is being presented here, I also know that there is one person who is willing to give insight and wisdom to anyone who asks. "If any of you lack wisdom, let him ask of God, that giveth to all *men* liberally, and upbraideth not; and it shall be given him." James 1:5.

Prayer:

Dear Lord, give our politicians enough wisdom to debate all bills in the interest of everyone concerned. Remind them that, they too, were once just an unborn baby. The reason they are able to stand up and make such an important contribution to our country is direct result of being born and growing up. They have all overcome the challenges that they faced during their childhood with a strength that brought them to this place in this time. May the children that they pass judgement on be able to, one day, stand beside them and make a similar contribution to the lives of future Australians.

My youngest child was visiting after I wrote this story, and the abortion issue was being reported on by someone on the Television. They said, "I don't know what the issue is, if a woman wants to abort her baby they should be allowed to". I stood up and as I walked out of the room replied, "And that's what the doctor suggested I do to you."

When I found out that I was pregnant with this child, I was getting close to 38 years old. I hadn't planned on getting pregnant, but I knew that our then youngest child could use a sibling closer to his age. There was a seven-year gap between the third and fourth child. When I told the doctor that I hadn't planned this one he just said we can do something about that if you want. I said NO.

It had nothing to do with my health or the health of the baby, it was an option because I hadn't planned to fall pregnant. I'd had multiple miscarriages so the possibility of me going full-term was remote. It's something that I rarely talked about and, in fact, I realised that it was probably the first time that I had told my child what the doctor said.

Two minutes later that child came and found me and said "Mum, I'm glad you didn't abort me." We then talked about how life wasn't easy for either of us. This child was the one that I had to drag kicking and screaming into adulthood and there were times when they were in very dark places. I pointed out that their partner's son, who he is raising as his own even though there is no genic connection, would have missed out on so much if I had aborted him and life would have been so much poorer without him. Yes, it's personal. My child changed their mind once they realised that their life on earth might not have been. I wonder how many of those who were advocating for this bill are only here because their mother said no, and never told anyone.

Please Bless the Bush

In a telephone interview during the drought, I was asked how the church should be praying for those suffering through intense drought. I don't normally do phone interviews, but because of the drought I hadn't been able to visit my family for over two years.

We talked about the drought and how it was affecting us. I asked that they pray for courage to go out each day and get through the daily grind of feeding stock and carting water and that people would visit the farmers and their families.

Why would I be asking for these things rather than help in the form of money?

While money and hay supplies are essential, and they really are, they don't reach everyone. Some farmers have been blessed enough to have stock feed in storage and are currently able to feed their stock, some just refuse to ask for help, and some just miss out because there aren't sufficient supplies to go around. These farmers were still facing the devastation of watching their pastures and stock die and their dams drying up on their own.

We have been told that we should be having conversations with each other to help our mental health. I was asked once why that wasn't already happening.

The answer is fairly simple. Farming today is a lonely occupation. We no longer need to borrow the neighbours' tractor or header like previous generations of farmers did. These farmers were already having conversations with each other during the good times while they worked together. So, the conversations were able to continue when the hard times arrived. Most farms employed more than just the family. Today, technology allows farmers to operate multiple pieces of machinery without the need to employ staff (this is what makes us so efficient) but it also means they can go weeks without speaking to another soul even in the good times. When droughts hit, the workload goes up and so does the loneliness.

I spoke to one farmer who was looking glum one day. Twenty minutes later they said that they were feeling much better and admitted that as they were driving between properties to feed stock, they had a lot of time to think and worry about how bad things were. Knowing that someone understood how tough things were made them feel better.

When you have a conversation with someone else, you often realise that there are many people out there who have just as many problems, or more, than you do and you can find things to thank God for but, more importantly, you realise that you are not going through this alone.

Statistics tell us that, each week, one farmer was committing suicide. When they feel alone, disrespected, and struggling with debt they often see this as the only way out. Frequently, they see the insurance payout as the only means that will allow their families to carry on doing what they love.

It's not just the farmers who are affected by drought or any major disaster, it's every small business and every town, large or small around which farms are situated. I watched a shopkeeper come close to tears because I had made the decision to buy an item with gifted money from their shop rather than buy the same item on the internet.

Come and visit a farmer, but don't bring your judgement, bring a willing heart to learn and understand. Things will not be rosy, they are devastating, they are not pretty, but farmers have to do what they do. Then I ask you to go home and get angry. Angry that things were not done in the past in order to make sure that things didn't get this bad and angry that if things aren't implemented now our children and grandchildren will also face these problems in the future.

This will bless the bush more than you will ever know.

Prayer:

Father, open the hearts of your people so that they are willing to learn how things are with their neighbours, our Australian farmers. Father, give each of us the courage to do what needs to be done to make sure that food is available to each and every person that lives in the great land that you brought us to over two hundred years ago. Forgive us for not preparing our country for such times as these and please be gracious to us and send us drought breaking rain across the whole of our land. Amen.

Prayer.

During October 2019, Christians in Australia were praying for God to send us drought breaking rain. Many parts of our country had been in drought from three to ten years by then. Many towns were running out of water and some towns had to truck water in for their residents.

So, during the month of October, I joined the multitude of prayers by looking at the four aspects of prayer. There were eight days of adoration, eight days of thanksgiving, eight days of repentance and seven days of petition.

However, it doesn't matter what we are praying for, we are able to apply this process of praying to any issue that needs our prayers, personal or communal.

Adoration

Day one: Lord, how great is your creation. You have blessed us with a wonderful place to live and we praise you.

Day two: Lord, how wonderful is the sky that you have spread across the whole world. Its blue is so restful for our eyes. Even when there are no clouds, it is beautiful.

Day three: Lord, we admire the parts of your creation that bloom even in the dry times.

Day four: Lord, we are amazed at how you have endowed people with many skills, and they are often only found during the tough times in our lives.

Day five: Lord, how great it is to wake to the sounds of birds singing. Their music makes us mindful of all the music that you have created.

Day six: Lord, your amazing creation is set to a pattern that you created, and you continue to hold that creation together each and every day.

Day seven: Lord you created the circle of life, birth, growth, death, it amazes me that you have allowed us to be part of that great circle.

Day eight: Lord, how amazing is it that you can see all things, the beginning and the end, which will go on into eternity.

Thanksgiving

Day nine: Thank you, for sending Jesus to die on the cross for my sins and writing my name in the book of life.

Day ten: Thank you for your word, that guides us as to how to live your way instead of our own way.

Day eleven: Thank you for the Holy Spirit that lives within us, giving us the courage to do what needs to be done each day and inspiring us with solutions to our problems.

Day twelve: Thank you for telling me in Psalm 139:16 that you knew me and the plan that you have for me, even before time began.

Day thirteen: Thank you for placing me in this particular time in history.

Day fourteen: Thank you, that you for allowing the technologies that keep us connected even when they frustrate us when they don't work like we expect them to.

Day fifteen: Thank you, Lord, for all the friends that pray for me in secret.

Day sixteen: Lord, thank you that no matter what we are going through, your creation gives us a sense of certainty, as the sun rises each morning and sets in the evening.

Repentance

Day seventeen: Lord, forgive me for all the small things that I do each day that dishonour your name.

Day eighteen: Lord, forgive me for all the times that I am ungrateful for your blessing of a new day just because the day before didn't go the way I wanted it to.

Day nineteen: Lord, forgive me for being ungracious when you ask me to put someone else's needs before my own.

Day twenty: Forgive my unthankful heart, help me to complain less and praise more for the blessings that you have given us even when I don't feel like it.

Day twenty-one: Forgive me for not trusting you, for letting my worries shut out your voice that tells me, you are always in control.

Day twenty-two: Forgive me for all the times I let my frustrations spill over and bring dishonour to your name.

Day twenty-three: Forgive me for all the times I point the finger at other's mistakes instead of looking at my own, even when I don't say anything.

Day twenty-four: Forgive us for all the times that we push you aside and try to fix things ourselves instead of waiting for your answer.

Petition

Day twenty-five: Please, Lord, give me more faith that I might trust you more and please send rain.

Day twenty-six: Please Lord, help me to honour you by not complaining when trials come to help me trust you more and send us rain.

Day twenty-seven: Please give me courage to tell others how much you love them and send life-saving rain.

Day twenty-eight: Genises 8:22 tells us that "While the earth remaineth, seedtime and harvest, and cold and heat, and summer and winter, and day and night shall not cease." Help us to accept that you have set this pattern and give us the wisdom to work within it and please send us rain.

Day twenty-nine: Please give us the wisdom to know when to wait and when to act, and the courage to do both, and give our Earth rain.

Day thirty: Please, Father, help those in power to have the courage to do the right thing for our country so that the world will see that you are the all-powerful God that you are, and bless us with rain.

Day thirty-one: Lord, we ask that you would, please, send rain for your thirsty country.

Prayers for Drought Breaking Rain

If you were to go to a service set aside to pray for rain, would you take an umbrella with you? Here are some prayers that I wrote during the worst drought in our living memory so far. However, physical drought isn't the only time when we come to God with desperate pleas for His intervention in our lives. This pattern was given to us by Jesus himself.

While the earth remaineth, seedtime and harvest, and cold and heat, and summer and winter, and day and night shall not cease. Genesis 8:22

Prayer of Adoration

Lord, you knew each and every one of us from before time began. You determined our seasons of Summer, Spring, Autumn, and Winter, the times of heat and cold, night and day, these are your determination, and we know that they are decreed for our benefit. You also gave us the skills that we have, and you have placed us in this time and space for your glory. Thank you, Lord.

Lord, only you can give the rain that this thirsty land needs. You are the God of creation, both the world and each person who lives in it, you are sovereign. Everything works according to the plans that you put in place at the beginning of time and no other. It is your good pleasure that allows us to be here and, Father, we honour you as the creator, saviour, and giver of all things. Thank you, Lord, as our maker, you alone determine the length of our days. Your great plan will be carried out according to your will and our part in it will be guided by your hand.

Prayer of Thanksgiving:

For the creation of our world and for giving us this great southern land and all the resources that it contains to use. For those surrounding seas that enable us to protect the biodiversity of our land. We thank you, Father. For the skills of our farmers as they work hard for many long hours each day. We thank you, Father. For the beauty of your sunrises and sunsets. For their families that support them and their children who adore them. We thank you, Father. For the times of prosperity that we have enjoyed in the past. For those that you placed in the right place at the right time and inspired to develop new technologies. We thank you, Father.

Prayer of Forgiveness

For all those times when we ignored you or failed to give you full credit for your handiwork and blessings. For the times we took your name in vain and called you Mother Nature. Forgive us, Father. For our arrogance in believing that we knew better than you and could change your blueprint for our world and took your goodness for granted. Forgive us, Father. For thinking of ourselves and not those who might be affected by our actions and allowing our fellow citizens to suffer. Forgive us, Father.

Prayer of Petition

Father, we ask that you would bless our thirsty land with rain. Rain that will soak down into the earth and allow our crops and pastures to grow again in the springtime. We pray, oh Lord, for those who you have set to rule over us, we pray that they will see our plight just as your eyes have seen it and that they will be moved with compassion and render assistance to all those in need. We pray, oh Lord, Father, that you will open our eyes and ears to any opportunity where we can give assistance. Please give us the strength and grace to put others' needs before our own. Fill us with inspiration, oh Lord.

Prayers of Blessing

Scrolling through the internet at any time is a blessing and a curse. There are many people who stand beside the Australian Farmers and small-town businesses particularly during times of intense drought. There are also those who blame, laugh, and tell us that our situation is hopeless. The ones who hurt the most, though, are those who laugh at the possibility that God is real and will one day send rain on this thirsty land.

God used these people one day to challenge me. While I was tempted to give some of these people the angry icon, (God forgive me, please) I scrolled past, shook my head, and ignored them.

A small quiet voice asked me, "What do I want you to do for those people. Those who curse you?"

"But I say unto you, Love your enemies, bless them that curse you, do good to them that hate you, and pray for them which despitefully use you, and persecute you; That ye may be the children of your Father which is in heaven: for He maketh his sun to rise on the evil and on the good, and sendeth rain on the just and on the unjust." Matthew 5:44-45.

As I try to be faithful to my Lord, I started that process of praying for all those who had made any comments that I didn't agree with. That voice kept going. "You have no idea of what they have been through that has shaped their lives, thinking patterns and emotional reactions".

To those people I say, please forgive me for not understanding your point of view. I will continue to pray for you. I thank those who are praying for us, the Australian farmers, small town residents, and the bush in general.

Prayer:

Lord, you are the Lord of Lords. We thank you for the way you have sustained us during this time of desperate need for rain.

We pray for those who do not believe you exist. We pray that you will bless them in a special way with no strings attached, Lord. I'm not asking that they will be able sympathise with us, that they will become friends with our farmers but Lord, the only thing that I ask that they too will know that You are the Lord of Lords and that they are loved by you no matter what they have been through at the hands of the one who would like to ruin this world. Forgive us for not seeing them as you see them.

Lord, we praise you for those who stand beside us and pray with us for all those going through times of trial. May you be glorified. Amen.

Praying Right

Are you ever surprised at how prayers are answered?

Many years ago, I had inherited a lounge suite from my grandmother. However, it was built for a sedate couple not an energetic family of five children. In a very short period of time, it disintegrated until I was left with one chair with one broken leg. Due to my sentimental attachment, I replaced the leg with a couple of bricks and used it as my place where I could read, pray, and generally have time to myself.

As the repair was so temporary there were several occasions when the chair would move and fall off the bricks. I spent a lot of time praying and fussing to God about the repairs that were needed on that chair and the rest of the suite. I wanted it to be restored to its original pristine condition.

One day after I had replaced it again back on the bricks, I stood in front of it and yelled at God (yes, God allows us to yell at Him) 'I just want it to be safe to sit in!'. As I look back at that prayer, I can now imagine that God let out a sigh and said 'Finally, she gets it'. Within minutes God reminded me that the other chair was in the shed, and I could use it to fix the one in the house. Which I did.

God had answered my prayer, not because I yelled at Him, although at the time I thought it was, but because I had finally asked for the right thing.

"And this is the confidence that we have in him, that, if we ask any thing according to his will, he heareth us: And if we know that He hear us, whatsoever we ask, we know that we have the petitions that we desired of him." 1 John 5:14-15.

Instead of telling Him what to do, I finally asked Him to give me a safe place to talk to Him.

Looking at my prayer life now, I find that I am still doing the same thing. Sadly, I have found that too often I'm telling Him that our situation will be fixed if He sends rain, if we can find a way to make money out of rocks (after that's all that's left on the ground as a result of the drought), if I sell enough books to buy feed for the sheep and the list goes on.

What should I be really praying for? God put me here in this wonderful land that He has blessed many times over since creation. Yes, things are not as good as they used to be, but they are still better than other places in the world. My prayer should be that God be glorified only. As with the chair, once we pray as God wants, we release our minds and imaginations to hear the answers that God has already prepared for us.

Prayer:

Oh Lord, forgive us for all the times we tell you how to fix our situations. Help us to remember that the reason you placed us here on earth was to worship you and that we should be praying that you will be glorified through all our circumstances both good and bad.

Praying with Faith

My microwave oven was showing its age. The clock display didn't work. When I punched in the time, I had to have faith that I'd pushed the correct numbers as there was no longer any visible confirmation available.

There is something about time. It seems to be flexible, in that there are times when it seems to race ahead and other times when it drags.

So, there were times when the microwave oven seemed to be running for longer than I expected, and I'd start to second guess myself and doubt if I really did punch in the correct time.

After second guessing myself once more, I was reminded of a time when we were praying for a new car. With the arrival of our third daughter, we needed to upgrade our car. We had a small Datsun 180B at the time and fitting two car seats and a bassinet on the back seat was pretty difficult. We had just had a large number of our stock stolen, so money was very tight for the day-to-day stuff, let alone a new vehicle. One of our friends upgraded their vehicle on a regular basis and offered us a couple of weeks to buy his current one. It was a Commodore and would have solved our space issues very nicely. However, the price that he was asking us to pay was way out of our reach. I remember distinctly saying to God that the only way we would be able to afford that vehicle was if we won the lotto. I didn't say anything to my husband, and I didn't go out and buy a ticket either, I just resigned myself with having to cope with the small car for a lot longer. A few weeks went past, and our friends dithered about whether they really wanted the new one. Now I cannot remember exactly how, I think the price of wool soared that year, but suddenly we had extra money. By the time our friends had actually decided that they were going to get the new model we had the money to buy their old car at the price that they had asked. Mum was visiting at the time when we took delivery of the vehicle and my husband said something really interesting. "This is just like winning the lotto only we have to pay tax on it". God knew where the money for the car was coming from all along and that we wouldn't need the lottery to make it happen. I'm sure that there would have been some awkward, long-lasting consequences had I taken things into my own hands, gone out and actually purchased a ticket, particularly if it had been a winner. Thankfully, I have never had to find out.

What is the connection between this past event and my microwave timer? It has to do with time. How many times do we pray for something, and it seems that God answers quickly, almost instantly and then there are times when we continue to pray and it seems that God takes a very long time to answer.

Like punching in the numbers on the microwave oven keypad, when we pray, we are asking in faith, without any visual confirmation that He has heard us, or He will answer in the way that we expect or desire.

Matthew 7:7 says: "Ask, and it will be given you. Seek, and you will find. Knock, and it will be opened for you."

Queen

Esther 2:12-15. 1 Cor 13:4-7.

As we celebrated the Queen's jubilee, I was thinking about how, when she was growing up, she had no expectation that she would one day have to rule over the commonwealth. After all her father had an older brother who was expected to carry out his duties as the next monarch. What I had become aware of, over the years was that as much as the royals have the freedom to do what they like, the rules appear to be very confining. Those in administration are the ones who dictate what can and cannot be done.

Yet, when Elizabeth was required to do her duty, she did it with a strong determination and strength that was remarkable.

When you think about it, there is another woman with whom Queen Elizabeth II had a lot in common with.

This woman, growing up, never ever expected to become queen. Her name was Esther. While, unlike Elizabeth II, she didn't have the role of ruler, she used her skills in order to save God's people and had many of the qualities that we understand our Queen to have. Let's have a look at what those qualities are:

1. Obedience (2:10, 15)
2. Pleasant/Friendly (2:9)
3. Wise enough to seek advice and follow it (2:10, 15, 20; 4)
4. Boldness – courage in action, despite realistic fear (4:16, 7:3)
5. Faith (5:4)
6. True humility (7:3-4, 8:1-2)

The other qualities that I see expressed in these verses are those listed in 1 Cor 13:4-7 and it's these qualities that I think made her attractive to those around her.

As women of God, we need to try and develop these qualities in ourselves. We are given those instructions in Ephesians 4:32, Mathew 5:43-48, Colossians 4:6 and Mathew 7:12 to name a few.

Given that her husband, King Xerxes, only reigned for 21 years she had no hope of having the extensive influence that Queen Elizabeth II has had, but her impact on the Jewish people was to be just as powerful.

Many of us find ourselves in positions that we never expected us to be in as children. We had our dreams and aspirations, some of us would have seen them realised but I expect that there are just as many of us who haven't.

However, did we accept those challenges with the same grace and tenacity that Queen Esther accepted hers?

Prayer:

Lord, where you lead, I'm willing to follow, but help me to follow with the grace and obedience that was shown by your servant Queen Esther, so that you may be honoured and people saved through your plan for each one of us.

Rattled

The trouble with being a sounding board for my family is that it sometimes leaves me rattled for a while afterwards.

The day before, I had listened to the concerns of one child, been frustrated by another, and the morning had brought a conversation with another in which I was reminded of the lasting effects of something that had happened some thirty years before. I've always been grateful that the results of that accident could have been a lot worse than they were, but I was still left with the feeling that I was never going to be forgiven for what had happened. On top of all this, I was sent a message about an event that would have been a dream fifteen years ago but is no longer possible. I was surprised at how, somewhere deep down inside me, I wanted to revive that dream but continued to quash it with all the obstacles that would have to be overcome. I was tired and rattled and yes, tears flowed.

I had a list of things that I needed to do, so I started to work my way through them, without any enthusiasm, adding a few more. After all, my day would only get worse if I didn't cross them off my list. I started to feel a bit better and while talking to the Lord as I was doing the dishes, He reminded me that He could move a mountain if I had faith as small as a mustard seed. Mathew 17:20. I was also reminded of, Romans 8:28, "All things work together for good to them that love God, to them who are the called according to his purpose."

His purpose for me, certainly at the moment, is to be here for my family. It doesn't seem to involve travelling around the world. I had to also remind myself that God was very capable of using all past events for my good and even the good of my family.

I can't see the "how" yet, but He can.

Reality Check

A lady with a lot going on in her life, rang me one day asking for prayer. She was feeling very overwhelmed with all that she had to cope with. I made the mistake of telling her that God wouldn't give her any more than what she could cope with (I should have known better), and she snapped back, "Well, God needs a reality check".

"There hath no temptation taken you but such as is common to man: but God *is* faithful, who will not suffer you to be tempted above that ye are able; but will with the temptation also make a way to escape, that ye may be able to bear *it*." 1 Corinthians 10:13.

I knew that what I had said, didn't help her, because others had said the same to me at times when I was feeling overwhelmed.

Praying for her a couple of days later, it occurred to me that it wasn't God who needed the reality check but the devil. He needed to be told that God is bigger than he is, greater than he is and way more powerful.

"These things I have spoken unto you, that in me ye might have peace. In the world ye shall have tribulation: but be of good cheer; I have overcome the world." John 16:33.

So, next time someone asks me to pray for them I will be more careful with my words, and remind those who are overwhelmed who is really the more powerful person in their lives.

Prayer:

God, sometimes it is easy to forget who the most powerful person in our world is when we are overwhelmed by the problems that come with living in this world. Help us all to remember that you are more powerful than anyone.

Reinvention

As part of the process of renovating my house, it has been necessary for me to restore and upscale some pieces of furniture.

As I scraped back, in some cases, layer after layer of paint, I thought about how many different uses they would have been put to over the years. After all, at some point most of them started out as pristine new pieces, with a certain purpose and look that suited the style of the day.

I'm sure, if they could talk, there would be some very interesting stories about the various owners who had used them, the repairs that had been carried out on them with different levels of skill, what had been stored inside or placed on them.

However, over the years, as damage, fashion and tastes changed, so did the look and use of the pieces. It was obvious in some cases that repairs had been carried out in a hurry, or with materials that were from something else because they didn't match. It wasn't hard to accept that some repairs would have been required during tough economic times and it was necessary to use whatever was on hand. In some cases, the look was changed simply by adding another layer of paint over a previous colour. One particular piece, I counted five different layers of paint.

It also occurred to me that in some ways these pieces of furniture have some parallels to our lives.

We move through life's stages, each stage has different challenges and trails, requiring new skill sets for us to overcome or meet them. But unlike all these pieces of furniture, who had a mirid of owners, all of whom had very different ideas about what the piece should look like and be used for, we only have one person who is in charge of the plan and repurposing of our lives, God.

Ecclesiastes 3:1-8 reminds us that there is a time for everything, some are very challenging to face, others are more enjoyable but through them all, God is with us, and will continue to support us because He is the constant factor in our lives.

Relationship

The older I get the more I realise that the quality-of-life correlates to the quality of our relationships with those around us. We all know that even the very best of relationships here on earth can be difficult at times. There are so many issues that need to be navigated, people's past experiences, health issues, emotional fluctuations, and the influence of the devil, to name a few, that make relationships hard work.

At Christmas time we celebrate the birth of Jesus. He came to earth as a baby, to grow up and share the trials and joys of our lives in order to reinstate our relationship with God. He has shown us how much God loves us and the lengths that He was willing to go to, to restore that bond between us and God.

Jesus also had to navigate His relationships with the disciples, their families, and the authorities that were constantly trying to tell him how He should behave. Peter was outspoken, John was just a youth with a lot to learn, John and James's mother wanted special treatment of her sons, Thomas had his misgivings, Judas always worried about the wrong things and none of them understood the process that would create His new kingdom. These people were just as complicated as we are to live with.

Thinking ahead to our lives in Heaven, I'm beginning to comprehend that its perfection will have a lot to do with the fact that all our relationships will be perfect, not only with God but with each other. It will be so nice to talk to someone and not have to worry about hidden agendas, misunderstandings, offending, being offended, or just being ignored. Oh, what bliss that will be.

However, in the meantime, let us ask the Holy Spirit to help us communicate with those around us in a way that will improve our relationships.

1 Peter 4:8 says: "And above all things be earnest in your love among yourselves, for love covers a multitude of sins."

Shards of Light

Have you ever been in the middle of a storm? The heavy black clouds creating a huge suffocating ceiling above you. Suddenly, the clouds part just a little, and in an instant the sunlight strikes the ground like a golden sword. You can only gasp at the beauty of it and give thanks that, above the storm, the sun is still there and will shine again once the storm has passed.

In life, we are always going to experience storms. Spiritual, emotional, physical, and environmental ones. Some are going to be more oppressive than others. There is a tendency to hunker down and wait the storms out. We may also feel that the storms will never end, and to some extent, that will be true. Storms will follow us until the day we go home to be with our Lord. Sometimes we just want to wrap ourselves up and stay out of harm's way.

Let's do that.

Let's be sure that we do wrap ourselves up, reading God's word and praying, communing with Christian family and know that He will protect us.

"He that dwelleth in the secret place of the most High shall abide under the shadow of the Almighty. I will say of the LORD; *He is* my refuge and my fortress: my God; in him will I trust." Psalm 91:1-2.

I was recently reminded that during each and every storm there will also be shards of light. Let's not hunker down so much that we miss these beautiful expressions of God's love for us.

Where are these shards of light in life's storms?

Did someone smile at you today? Did you find a flower out in full bloom? These are shards of light. There are the bigger ones as well. Someone has a car accident and only breaks their little finger. Rain falls on a drought ravished paddock, it's not enough but it's better than nothing. There are so many and for each of us they will all be different.

Yes, we live in a very bleak world but let's also keep our eyes open to see the wonderful things that God is doing around us, because He is the one that is in control and He has our best interests laid firmly on His heart.

"And Jesus came and spake unto them, saying, All power is given unto me in heaven and in earth." Matthew 28:18.

"Who (Jesus) has gone into heaven and is at the right hand of God, with angels, authorities, and powers subject to Him." 1 Peter 3:22.

Are you watching for those wonderful shards of light in your storm?

Sharing

'I have heard about your faith', Paul writes to the church of Ephesus to encourage them. He was, according to tradition, locked away in a Roman Prison. He was unable to visit these people no matter how badly he would have liked to.

His information about what was happening in this church, which he had helped to establish, had been delivered by messengers.

What he heard encouraged him enough for him to give thanks to God for the love that they showed for all the saints, and I think that the love they showed probably went out to the whole church including those in Rome.

Their knowledge of the churches around the world at that time would have been delivered by the many messengers that travelled back and forth, criss crossing the world.

Each year, as we meet for our World Day of Prayer, we also get to hear about the faith of those who are far away from us geographically, using the services that they have put together. While the method is different, the effect is much the same. We have heard of their faith, their struggles, some of the problems unique to their culture.

We have heard the special stories of the ladies that have been brave enough to share their own particular circumstances.

Unlike Paul, most of us will never have the opportunity to visit these countries, but we still have this very special chance to find out about how our brothers and sisters serve the same Lord we do.

Let us imagine for a moment that the church of Ephesus only held a service once a year to hear about the other churches around them. It would have been hard for Paul to hear about their faith, and their issues. He heard because they were willing to share with everyone who passed through their town.

Yet, here at home, how do others hear about our faith.

We don't put together a service each year, and if we did, would that be enough? For others to hear about our faith, just like the church of Ephesus, we need to share it with those who we interact with every day, not just one day a year.

So, how do we make sure that others hear of our faith? The first and most effective way of making sure others know about our faith, is to live it, by always being willing to show others the love of God by carrying out acts of service, with an honest and diligent attitude.

For example, I read a story about someone showing the love of God. They collected the rubbish bins as an act of service, and they always washed them out. Even though it was such a small thing, it got the attention of the shop owner and led to her asking about why he did it. This small thing gave him the opportunity to share about God. May we all look for those small moments in our own lives.

Sheltered

A patch in my backyard was bugging me. The grass looked untidy, so it was time to get the mower out and do something about it. The weather had been dry and hot for several weeks and the ground had cracked open, something our soil does as it dries out. What I noticed was that, where the grass was sheltered by the house or even just a garden bench, it had grown a lot more despite the large cracks in the ground.

I was reminded of something very important. It doesn't matter how big the cracks in our lives are, whether it is sickness, drought, unemployment, family disfunction, or government stupidity, if we are sheltering under the wings of God we will continue to grow. There will be times when that growth will be slower than others, but it will still be there and we are better off than those who refuse to come to Jesus for shelter.

Psalm 36:7 says: "How precious is your loving kindness, God! The children of men take refuge under the shadow of your wings."

Isaiah 41:10 says: "Fear thou not; for I *am* with thee: be not dismayed; for I *am* thy God: I will strengthen thee; yea, I will help thee; yea, I will uphold thee with the right hand of my righteousness."

Yes, the world seems to have a lot of cracks in it these days, and it can be easy to look at them and wonder how soon one might open up right under you and make you fall, but even in the midst of that, God will be there.

Prayer:

Thank you, Lord, for reminding me that no matter how bad things look around me, you have me covered and no matter what my circumstances are you are helping us to grow closer to you.

Shingles

The pain was coming and going like waves crashing against the rocks, yet I tried to explain it away. I'd eaten something I shouldn't have, or hadn't eaten something I should have, I'd been sitting too long without enough exercise.

I found a small blister in the middle of my chest; I explained that away as I must have been bitten by something. The pain was in my back, the "bite" on my chest, the two could not be related.

With a family history of gall bladder issues, it was considered the most likely of explanations as the pain was in the right place, but after a week, it was starting to exhaust me. What I couldn't collate was that the pain attacks happened in the middle of the night, not always after I'd eaten, though that happened enough times for it to still be gall related.

I was staying with family, and I wanted to be considerate, they worked hard and had very busy lives, they didn't need to be disturbed by some pain, or a simple bite.

I also had a function to attend and as I had missed the last big event, I cried to God that I wouldn't miss this one. God heard my prayer, and I got through the day, with very little pain.

The bite started to spread and after a week, I showed it to my sister, an ex-nurse, who said that it should be seen to. The pain seemed to be going away, so it almost seemed pointless to mention it, until I got in the car to go to the hospital, and then it started to ramp up.

The nurse at the hospital asked about if I'd ever had problems with anti-depression medication, something I wasn't keen to explore because I have such a list of allergies, a very long list. The word shingles wasn't mentioned until change over, when a nurse suggested it was a possibility, the admitting nurse replied that it was one of the things being considered.

Three doctors later, and the diagnosis was confirmed, but I decided that I wanted to continue to just use the Panadol for my treatment. Such is my fear of new medications. Two days later and I wasn't coping. The pain was making me feel sick and the pain killers were taking a long time to kick in. Back to the hospital we went and another doctor, who showed great sympathy and understanding, gave me an alternative treatment, which I accepted when they agreed to supervise me for a while to make sure that I wouldn't have an adverse reaction.

Throughout it all, I knew many people were praying for my recovery, and I know that, like many other times, particularly when the children were small, when I have had other illnesses that could have been very debilitating, He has blessed me with only a mild case which has enabled me to carry on doing what I needed to.

God has proved to me over and over that He wouldn't give me more than I could handle. Even if sometimes I have doubted my ability to cope.

1 Corinthians 10:13 says, "No temptation has taken you except what is common to man. God is faithful, who will not allow you to be tempted above what you are able, but will with the temptation also make the way of escape, that you may be able to endure it."

Skill Shortage

I must admit to enjoying a series of stories about a certain character with some very special gifts, but the thing that I admired most about this character was her ability to point people in the right direction, particularly when something needed to be done, and allowed them to take all the credit.

If there was a skill that I would like to develop, it would be that one. Yet, my human nature fights me all the time on this very thing. When I help people and don't get any credit for my part in the process, I feel slighted.

Paul also had this problem, it seems: "For I don't know what I am doing. For I don't practice what I desire to do; but what I hate, that I do. But if what I don't desire, that I do, I consent to the law that it is good. So now it is no more I that do it, but sin which dwells in me. For I know that in me, that is, in my flesh, dwells no good thing. For desire is present with me, but I don't find it doing that which is good. For the good which I desire, I don't do; but the evil which I don't desire, that I practice. But if what I don't desire, that I do, it is no more I that do it, but sin which dwells in me." (Romans 7:15-20).

In 2 Corinthians 12:9 Paul writes, after asking God to remove some weakness that he had, whether it was physical or emotional we have no idea, "And he (God) said unto me, My grace is sufficient for thee: for my strength is made perfect in weakness.

Most gladly therefore will I rather glory in my infirmities, that the power of Christ may rest upon me."

It's a good thing that God understands our frailty as humans, and because He is all powerful, is willing to help us through any struggle and will help us to develop any skills that we need.

What are you asking God to help you with?

Taking up the Batton

I was reminded of the fact that we are only managers of this world for a very short time. We came into the world without any knowledge of what we can, would, or could do. We have to learn how to sit, walk, run, and talk. What and how we learn will shape what God wants us to do with our time before He passes the job onto someone else to carry on.

We have seen this many times in the farming industry, one parent has worked hard, built up their holding only to find that their offspring are not willing to carry it on, so it gets sold off and someone else gets to do the hard work of starting again, or it goes to a big corporation that doesn't acknowledge all the hard work that went into the holding.

I've often been saddened, having read about the amazing work carried out by someone for God, only to find out that no one took up the batton after their time was finished. I've always felt that God had someone lined up to take up the work, and for some reason they have exercised their free-will and decided that they didn't want the load.

Have you ever wondered what would have happened if Joshua had decided that he would not be able to lead the people of Israel into the promised land. Maybe Caleb would have had to lead them home.

"Whereas you don't know what your life will be like tomorrow. For what is your life? For you are a vapor that appears for a little time, and then vanishes away." (James 4:14).

We see the truth of this every day, our lives can be changed in an instant, by illness, an accident, meeting someone, or a new job to name a few. That doesn't mean that we have to stop working for God. He may have a new or different direction that He wants us to take in order to serve Him.

When we feel that God wants us to take up the batton that someone else has been carrying for a long time, it is easy to feel unqualified, however, it has often been said that God doesn't call the qualified but qualifies the called, but this often happens after we have answered His call. It's the ultimate on-the-job training.

Let's do the best we can, to make the best of our lives and serve God faithfully, while we are able.

Tapestry

After her death, I acquired a latch hook rug project that my mother-in-law had started. It was something that I had always wanted to try and could never afford to do before they went out of fashion. To complete the project, you are required to take a two-inch piece of wool, which is supplied, and hook it through a hole, knotting it so that it stays in place. The colour that you used should match the colour faintly painted onto the background as a guide.

A few mornings later, I was listening to Psalm 139 and was reminded about how God knows, not only all about our lives, but the whole of our history from beginning to end. There is nothing about our entire world that God doesn't know.

I thought about how the rug project has the pattern painted onto the background fabric. It made me think about how our world's history is a bit like that background pattern, it's all there, God has it all planned out, and as time moves along, we are the pieces of wool that are used to make that pattern to come to life.

We cannot see the entire pattern, but God can, and He knows exactly which person will be the best match for each part of His pattern. Given that He will not force us to give up our own freewill, just like there are several pieces of wool the same colour, there are also others who can fill the position if we refuse to take part in God's best plan.

When our history is over and we get to see the final pattern, I'm sure that we will be very surprised at just how colourful and beautiful that pattern was, because I understand that most of us struggle to see how we fit into the bigger picture of things.

Prayer:

God, thank you for loving us and having the whole of history's plan worked out. Give us the courage to take our place in that plan.

Tears

We had tried everything that we knew to solve a problem, and nothing seemed to work. The day came when our hopes of solving it in a certain way had come to an end. As I said goodbye to that particular dream, the tears flowed. I was very sure that God wanted us to carry out the mission we had embarked on, and in my head, I knew that He had a solution, He just wasn't ready to show us what it was at this precise moment.

As the tears continued to flow, I asked myself a question. Was it wrong for me to cry when I knew that God had something better in store for us? Did my tears show a lack of faith in God's goodness?

The first thing I remembered was that Jesus cried at the tomb of Lazarus, but I felt that Jesus had cried because he knew that Lazarus was, at that moment, in a better place and would have to return to endure more trials and burdens that are part of our earthly journey.

The next thing that God whispered to me was that I had cried when I lost my mother, even though I knew that she was in Heaven and that I would see her again. This wasn't wrong, I knew that. So, why did I think that tears in this situation would be wrong?

I was still feeling grief, the dream that we had was being trampled on by greedy, hardheaded business people. We weren't being selfish or unreasonable in the offers that we had made, but we also needed to stay true to ourselves by standing by the decisions that we felt were right for us. The Bible tells us in Matthew 5:37 "But let your 'Yes' be 'Yes,' and your 'No,' 'No.' For whatever is more than these is from the evil one." By being undecisive we would be dishonouring to God.

Tears can help us heal. We experience grief on a lot of different levels, so feel free to cry, but remember that God has an answer, then, when you have cried, wipe your face, stand stall, and wait for God to show you what He has in store for you.

Thankfulness in Dry Times.

Do you find it hard to be thankful in the dry times of your life?

As the drought kept biting into the lives of so many of our farmers here in Australia (one farmer a week is committing suicide) we find it hard to find things to be thankful for. We hadn't had good rain for three years and forecasters were predicting another dry summer.

The questions we keep asking ourselves are: What should we be doing differently? How can we supplement our income? What happens if we run out of water? What happens when we run out of money to buy feed for the sheep? How long will it be before we get good rainfall again? And finally, how do we survive until our income starts to pick up after it does rain? After all, when it rains, it only rains water, not money. It takes at least two years or more to get your stock numbers back to where you can actually sell some.

So, when I think about the hot summer to come, I also thought about three other men who had to endure extreme heat. They were of course, Shadrach, Meshach, and Abednego. No-one has been through a fire that hot and survived to tell their story, except, they did.

Why?

They put God first and determined that they would worship Him and Him alone, regardless of how angry or devious people were around them.

They still had to go through the fire. God could have saved them and those who lost their lives during the preparations for their punishment.

No matter who we are, we have troubles in this world and the Lord will not always save us from having to walk through them, but He will walk with us and protect us just as He did for Shadrach, Meshach, and Abednego.

"Know therefore that the LORD thy God, he *is* God, the faithful God, which keepeth covenant and mercy with them that love him and keep his commandments to a thousand generations;" Deuteronomy 7:9.

I am thankful that God is keeping us through all our droughts. It's not to shield us from the dry times, it's not to keep all our stock alive, it is to help us to do what we must do each day and to do the best that we can with the resources that we have.

We can thank Him for the many blessings that we do have. We have water (Many around us don't), feed, even if it's not the grasses that the sheep need more than anything we can feed them, and not all of them have perished.

I want to say like Shadrach, Meshach, and Abednego "If it be *so*, our God whom we serve is able to deliver us from the burning fiery furnace, and he will deliver *us* out of thine hand, O king. But if not, be it known unto thee, O king, that we will not serve thy gods, nor worship the golden image which thou hast set up." Daniel 3:17-18.

Yes, our world has set up many golden images, money, sport, even climate change. If we don't pay homage to these things we are frowned upon and even jailed.

It's hard, but stay faithful, and God will give you small things to be thankful for until the big things happen.

The Blame Game

After another discussion about the pro and cons of replacing or repairing another old farm building that had been partly demolished by previous owners, I started to think about how many times we are left to clean up other's mistakes.

It's frustrating, but it's been happening since the 'fall'. For all have sinned, and come short of the glory of God; Romans 3:23.

The ultimate act of fixing others' mistakes, and our mistakes, was shown by Jesus, himself. He died on the cross to give us salvation from our sins.

It doesn't matter how careful we are about the way we live; the next generation will also be making up for the things that we did that cause issues in their world, just as we are doing the same now. I am so often reminded that I didn't live in those particular times in history and, if I'm honest, I have to admit that I most likely would have behaved in the same manner.

There have been so many times when I have wanted to turn back the clock and do things differently or even wished that others had done things differently. Yet, time, like the rain, is controlled by God.

The reality is that no matter what we do, it is going to cause issues for future generations. That is just the truth of being a human being. There's not a thing we can do about it.

I find it so easy to moan about these things or even worse, stand in judgement. I'm reminded that Jesus doesn't moan about the effort it took to fix up the mess we make of our lives. Just like He didn't judge the woman caught in adultery, John 8:1-11.

If I'm to be a true disciple of Jesus, then I should ask for the grace that He extended to me, and not moan or judge, but offer it to those in my present and my past.

Only when I let go of them can I focus clearly on the work in front of me. To walk my walk with love and a caring spirit and use what gifts He has endowed me with to solve the problems that are currently mounting around me, and leave the future and the past, where it really belongs, in God's Hands.

Prayer:

Father, we have many challenges facing us today. Forgive us for playing the blame game and give us the grace to let go of all the times when we think we, or others, have been wronged and focus on the job at hand with the same grace that you extended to the whole human race by dying on the cross. Help us to not only use the good brains you gave us but also your inspiration to find solutions to the problems we are faced with and then use your strength to get the job done.

The Feast

Luke 14:15-24

Verses 16-20. Here we have a parable about a man who has invited many of his wealthy friends to a feast. When he sends out his servant to tell them that all is ready, he discovers that they are not interested in attending; they have other things to do that are more important. One has a field to inspect, another has oxen to test out, and another has just got married so cannot attend.

I wonder what these things would look like in our day and age. Yes, the first one is simple. The field is still property, whether it be a house, farm, a business, even a new boat. Next, we have some oxen, what are oxen in the 21st century? Some will say that it's simple, farm machinery. But oxen were a means of making an income. So, they symbolise our work, regardless of what that might be, and finally the man who has just got married is putting family first. It could be said that this gentleman actually had a legitimate excuse as Deuteronomy 24:5 says: "When a man hath taken a new wife, he shall not go out to war, neither shall he be charged with any business: *but* he shall be free at home one year, and shall cheer up his wife which he hath taken."

These people, by refusing to attend the banquet, tell the host that he and his generosity is of no consequence.

So, instead of wasting the food, our host invites the poor, not just those we might think are poor because they haven't got a job, but those who are lonely and friendless for whatever reason. Connecting with those around us gives a richness that no money can buy and yet in this day and age, people are getting poorer than ever on this level.

What struck me recently was this; these people were also busy. They were not just sitting around waiting for someone to come and invite them to a feast or to make their lives better. Let's remember these people were outcasts, they would never expect something like that to ever happen. These were people who knew that if they are going to survive, they had to work harder and longer than the other formally invited guests.

Yet, when they are invited, they stopped what they are doing. They put it down. It wasn't so important; they were willing to leave it and enjoy the fellowship of others and their host. You and I also know that there would have been some of these individuals who would have turned down the invitation because they felt so unworthy, or too proud to attend. Yes, we can be proud of being an outcast. Pride can make us unwilling to accept charity, kindness, or in this case a good meal.

We have known right from the start that the host represents Christ Jesus, He is the one offering us the feast in Heaven for eternity. We also know that the people offering excuses are those who think that they don't need to accept that invitation. They will get to Heaven on their own merits, or they would never be good enough to be there. Either way, they are wrong.

How do these people relate to those we meet each day?

What do lame people look like in our society today? There are those who are hurting, abused, and depressed. They are held back by fear. These things make it hard for them to move forward in life and everything that they do can be a real effort.

Well, I am sure we all know someone who is blind. I'm not talking about the people who need a white stick or guide dog either. Most of those people have a greater insight into life than anyone who can see. The blind people that I am referring to are those who don't want to see any good in others, any beauty in the darkest of places, or any hope in the future.

Jesus offers the gift of salvation to all of us, the good, the bad, the ugly, and the beautiful. We are all equal in His sight. He created us, each one with our own unique DNA.

If you haven't accepted His gift yet, what is holding you back? Is what you have accumulated more important? Are you afraid that God is going to ask you to give it all up? Yes, he might! But ask yourself this; You can't take your house, farm, business, or boat with you when you die. These things are not going to comfort you even if you believe that there is nothing out there. You certainly can't take money with you, there is nothing to buy anyway.

The Bible tells us that there are two places in the hereafter, Heaven, and Hell. We are told that Hell is the loneliest place ever, and it will stay that way for eternity. So, your family will not be able to comfort you either.

Don't get me wrong, all these things are good in their right place, but we should not let them stop us from having a relationship with Jesus that will last forever.

Sometimes, others might think that your priorities are in the wrong place. Many years ago, my father was doing some contract hay baling. He had a family that needed to be fed, clothed, and schooled.

If you know anything about making hay, there are a few things that have to work together to make it a good product. It has to be cut at just the right time and dried to just the right level of moisture. If it's too damp, it will get hot and can even burst into flames. If it's too dry it doesn't pack tight in the bales effectively. In those days there were no chemical treatments to help, you were completely dependent on the weather to get it right. If you had really hot days the cut hay would be dry very quickly, if it rained you had to wait until it was dry again. Things had to work together, and they did to their own timetable. So, it turned out that my father had a string of weekends when he needed to cut or bale hay on a Sunday. Someone was bold enough to suggest that his priorities where a little out of whack. My father's reply in essence was that these farmers were paying him to cut and bale their hay. If it was ruined because he went to church, not only would they be pretty mad at him, but it would reflect badly on the church and God. I would guarantee you that cutting that hay did not interfere with my father's relationship with God. I'm sure that while he was cutting, raking, and baling, he was also having very long conversations with God.

Have you refused the invitation because you believe that God cannot love you because you are too bad, dirty, or unlovable? This parable is here to tell you that you are acceptable to Jesus, He wants you to accept His gift. Don't let pride stop you from walking into the most perfect place in all existence when your time here on earth is finished.

The Bible tells us in 1 John 1:9 "If we confess our sins, he is faithful and just to forgive us *our* sins, and to cleanse us from all unrighteousness."

Are you going to enjoy a feast in Heaven or are you letting something get in the way because you think it's too important?

Remember, nothing and no one is going to be able to comfort you in eternity, except Jesus. He is the one who will determine if you go to Heaven or Hell, and that will depend entirely on how you respond to His invitation of salvation.

The Sun

It was a rare cold morning in the middle of summer. As I woke up, the sun was shining through my window and warmed my face. I lay there, with my eyes closed, enjoying its warmth and part of a song started to run through my mind, "Look full into his face and the things of this world will grow slowly dim".

What I noticed was that I only had to move slightly, and the sun would be covered by the struts of the window frame. This reminded me that it doesn't take much for us to move away from the warmth of God's love, it doesn't mean that He isn't there, we just lose sight of it because we have moved away.

I was also aware that it wouldn't be long before the sun would rise higher into the sky, it's a natural thing that it does every day, that would also mean that I wouldn't be able to feel its warmth while I stayed in my bed, but again, it would still warm my world around me.

It's a bit like when life becomes hard with the challenges that we all have to face, it may seem as if God is hiding from us, yet He isn't, He is still there, it's just that earthly life sometimes gets in the way.

Just like we cannot look directly at God, I couldn't look directly at the sun but like the warmth that I could feel, I was again reminded that God's love, power, and grace is ever present.

Isaiah 41:10 says: "Fear thou not; for I *am* with thee: be not dismayed; for I *am* thy God: I will strengthen thee; yea, I will help thee; yea, I will uphold thee with the right hand of my righteousness."

This too will pass.

Another lockdown, more plans thrown out the window. The time of stress was stretching out well into its second year. As I woke to another day of not being sure of what I could or would be allowed to do, my heart cried 'this seems as if it's going to go on forever'.

God said, what did your mother tell you was the most common phrase in the Bible?

"And it came to pass," was my reply.

And so, it will!

Remember how people thought that WWII would be over by Christmas, they had to wait six years for it to end, and yet, it came to pass. How many times during those six years did people make the same cry of 'how long, Oh Lord?'

When God created the world, he created seasons: summer, winter, autumn, and spring. He gave us similar seasons in life, babyhood, childhood, youth, adulthood, and old age. All these seasons have their purpose and so it is with life. There are the good times and the bad times. Do you say that nature has abandoned itself in the winter season? No, we know that it is preparing for spring. If we accuse God of abandoning us in the bad times, we are saying that He isn't God, because those seasons in our lives are there to help us grow in faith, compassion, and as a community.

Romans 8:28 says: *"We know that all things work together for good for those who love God, to those who are called according to his purpose."* I have to remember that this verse says: **ALL THINGS**. It doesn't say that good things work, it means all things, the good, the bad, and the ugly. Yes, it's hard to see how, but one day we will. Yes, this season may have to pass before we can, but as God reminded me this morning, this too, will pass.

Prayer:

Lord, help us to understand that you are with us in the good, the bad, and the ugly of our world. Remind us constantly that nothing on earth will last forever and that includes this season of stress, sickness, and hardship. Help us to grow in the good things that you would want for us: faith, compassion, and a connected community. Amen

Turning our Eyes to Heaven

We are all equal in the eyes of God and He wants to let us know that He loves us equally.

Scripture:

That ye may be the children of your Father which is in heaven: for he maketh his sun to rise on the evil and on the good, and sendeth rain on the just and on the unjust. Matthew 5:45.

For the wages of sin is death, but the free gift of God is eternal life in Christ Jesus our Lord. Romans 6:23.

For thou shalt worship no other god: for the LORD, whose name *is* Jealous, *is* a jealous God: Exodus 34:14.

For whoever keeps the whole law and yet stumbles in one point, he has become guilty of all. James 2:10.

For the LORD your God *is* God of gods, and Lord of lords, a great God, a mighty, and a terrible, which regardeth not persons, nor taketh reward: Deuteronomy 10:17.

Our country was once known as the Great Southern Land of the Holy Spirit, but we have been pushing God out of our lives for so many years now. We even decided to take His name out of our National Anthem back in 1974. We have allowed our society to set up many great statutes of gold, these are anything that comes between us and God. Well, one's called 'climate change'. We have allowed this god to put the welfare of animals and the environment before people and our service to God. We even think that our actions, good and bad, can change something that God has complete control over.

When ignored by people who we want to engage with, we make sure that we get their attention. I'm sure most parents have unplugged the Xbox, TV, or computer in order to get the attention of their children. Bosses and adults use other methods to get the attention of fellow workers. I've seen teachers use some very creative methods to get the attention of their class.

God wants our attention. He wants us to talk to Him, love Him, engage with Him in praise of His goodness and His creation. Yet, we have collectively as a country failed to do this for so long. Is it any wonder that He has unplugged the very thing that we worship? He has stopped the rain, the thing that is essential to our lives and food, our very existence.

As our eyes constantly turn to the sky to wait for the clouds to form and pour out rain upon the dry, dusty earth beneath our feet, may we also fall on our knees and pray that God will forgive us for all the times we didn't remember that He is the creator, maintainer, and controller of our world. The one thing about drought, it doesn't discriminate between the rich, poor, guilty, or innocent. A great reminder that we are all equal in the eyes of our God.

When we return to giving the Lord of creation the respect, honour, and glory that is due to Him, then He will open His hand and pour spiritual and physical blessings out on our land.

Prayer:

Lord, we have grieved you for so long, we thank you for your patience, for the way you have continually blessed us even though we have been a thankless nation. Lord, forgive us for our thanklessness, forgive the way that we have treated our farmers, your servants, who work tirelessly. Lord, may your Holy Spirit move amongst all of us, stir us to tear down the gods we have replaced you with. We praise you for loving us all equally and Father we ask that you will open your hand and pour out great blessings once again on this your land, your great land. We plead that while we wait for your glorious physical redemption, that will bring glory to your name, that you will give each and every person waiting courage, strength, and wisdom to do the things that need to be done each and every day. Lord God, you are the creator of Heaven and Earth, that is true just as gravity holds us on it. No amount of denial will change you or your plans for our country but Father, we know that you want us to listen to you, talk to and praise you and Father, we know that sometimes you have to take drastic measures in order for us to sit up and take notice. So, Father, we know that you will pour rain down on our thirsty land in your own time because you have made us, and you know just how essential water is, not only to our land, but to our bodies. Amen.

Waiting

I had been putting off doing a particular job I had lined up for the morning because I didn't want to start and get interrupted by a phone call that I was expecting. The call was important for some other project. After waiting for over an hour and a half, I was beginning to think they weren't going to call. It wasn't hard to imagine that the caller had been called out on some emergency, after all, life happens to all of us from time to time, and while I worked on another project that could be easily interrupted, I found myself getting inpatient. I didn't have their number so I couldn't do anything else but wait for them to call me.

I was reminded during the process that God makes us wait, not only for His return but for many of the things that we ask of Him in prayer, for our daily lives, and waiting is hard.

We are not alone, there are so many people recorded in the Bible and history who have had to wait years for answers to their prayers. Some of them even decided not to wait but to try and make things happen by taking matters into their own hands with very long-lasting consequences.

In Psalm 40, David remembers all the good things that God had done for him while he was waiting for God to hear his cry.

Yes, waiting is hard, particularly when we feel that we need something desperately, or we are backed into a corner, but while we are waiting, let us remember the good things God has already done for us. We may have to write them down to help us remember them.

Wanted Qualities

Have you ever had a sibling or friend who had qualities you wanted in your life but didn't have? Did being around them make you feel sad or inadequate. Maybe you felt annoyed in the same way Joseph's brothers were annoyed with him.

Most people, I think, would put Joseph down as the original spoilt brat. After all, he was his father's favourite son. He was given special clothes and privileges. However, I was thinking about him recently and realised that if we look at what he was able to achieve later in life, albeit with the help of God, there was a lot more to him as a boy.

After all, he didn't say "Oops my brothers hate me, I had better become a better person." He just decided to be a hard worker when he was sold to Potiphar. He didn't decide to be honourable in order to be allowed to go home.

These were qualities that he had even as a child. Yes, he had an arrogant streak, but then I have a feeling that most of us have various amounts of that in our personalities.

Here was a boy who was intelligent, honest, and hard-working and I think that his telling of his dreams to his brothers was probably just the thing that tipped the scales. In other words, he was already showing them up because he was making the most of his abilities. He had what they wanted, and it annoyed them that they were not able to measure up.

The Old Testament is a pointer to Jesus. Recently, thoughts about the childhood of Jesus have been doing the rounds.

What was it like to be Jesus' Earthly mother?

Can you imagine telling any of your children to do something and have them go and do it without complaint and never throwing a tantrum because you said no to something they wanted? Mary had that! What a blessing.

On the other hand, can you see how difficult it would have been for his Earthly brothers and sisters. Did Mary let it slip in a time of frustration, "Why can't you be more like Jesus"? While there is no hint that he was given special privileges, it still would have made them crazy to try and reach His standards and consistently fail. Oh, how they must have smiled when Jesus stayed behind in Jerusalem. I pretty sure they thought His time to be punished had arrived.

One of the things that I envied Jesus for when I was a child, yes, I admit it, was His ability to see the real meaning behind the questions that were put to Him. This meant that He had the right answer every time. I never seemed to get it right when people tried to trip me up with silly questions. Oh, the frustration I felt!

There is good news! Since the death and resurrection of Jesus, the coming of the Holy Spirit and because I have asked Jesus to be part of my life, He is slowly changing me. It's His work in my life that is helping me to reach those things that I see in Him and other followers that I want in my life.

"Therefore, if any man *be* in Christ, *he is* a new creature: old things are passed away; behold, all things are become new." 2 Corinthians 5:17.

Would you like this too? Then ask Jesus to help you.

Watching Sheep

Have you ever watched how sheep behave? The more I watch, the more I see the same behaviours in people.

In Australia we farm sheep in a very different manner to how they do in the Middle East and how it was carried out in the Bible.

"He shall feed his flock like a shepherd: he shall gather the lambs with his arm, and carry *them* in his bosom, *and* shall gently lead those that are with young." Isaiah 40:11.

Because our flocks comprise of much larger numbers, thousands, rather than hundreds, it's inefficient to lead them, the flock or mob (as we call it), is pushed from the back. We have always done this, first with horses and now mostly with motor bikes. Some still lead from the front with the dogs following behind.

During good times, they are left in a paddock to feed on the pastures that are available and the grazier will check on them once or twice a day, tending to any specific health needs that they might have. It doesn't mean that he is not interested in their welfare he trusts that they will be able to get sufficient feed by themselves.

If a person tries to walk amongst them during these times, they very quickly run in the opposite direction.

During droughts, however, it's a very different proposition. The farmer must supply their requirements. This is usually carried out by pouring grain of some description from the back of the farm vehicle. At our place it's a two-person operation as someone has to drive while the other ensure that the feed is placed where the sheep can get access to it. Some farmers have feeders on the back of their utes, so it's a one-person operation.

It is during these times that sheep can be led. They come running when they hear the vehicle, even if it is just driving past between feed times. Even managing to get them into the sheep yards is faster if one person walks in front. They follow, when once they would have run away.

So, do I behave like a sheep?

As I watch them, I see so many times when I have behaved in the same manner. When things are good, I'm often far too content to soak up all the blessings that God sends my way. There are times when I try to do things my own way and ignore my master's voice when He calls me to a task that might require something a little difficult. However, when things get tough and it seems that all those great blessings have dried up, I, like the sheep, go running to my master. I follow Him around like my life depends on it, which it does of course.

"The name of the LORD *is* a strong tower: the righteous runneth into it, and is safe." Proverbs 18:10.

Oh, how I wish that I could remember to not be a sheep and be so dependent on the Lord, even when times are good.

What does Grown Up Australia Look Like

The debate about removing the Lord's Prayer from parliament was being aired on a News Channel. One commentator concluded that Australia needed to grow up and stop depending on prayer. Well, he is partly right, Australia does need to grow up. We are a young country but there is a big difference between growing older and growing up.

One would expect that while we age, we develop wisdom and maturity, however, this is not a natural occurrence in the aging process. As individuals age, the natural process means that our skin gets softer, hair turns grey, muscles ache, and bones start to creak. Mature behaviour doesn't come with the years we live but with how we live. It's worked on and developed.

The more mature we become, the more we realise that we cannot control what happens around us, the universe is much bigger and greater than we are, and that we really are only one small speck on the surface of the world, we know virtually nothing, we don't need to show off how rich or poor we are, making a big noise doesn't achieve very much, no-one is looking at us or interested in our opinion and whatever we have we cannot take it with us into the next world.

If you look at the mature people in this world, you will find that they don't try to tell you how rich or poor they are, they see a problem and get on with fixing it quietly, even if it is a mess that someone else created, with what resources they have and leave what they can't do for some other mature person to do the same. These are the real grownups.

So, what about a grown-up Australia.

I believe we were more mature before we started trying to show off to the rest of the world, how much wealth this country has, when we cared about our neighbour and the poor. When families came before work but at work, we gave it our all and dealt honestly with each other.

Yes, I know that not everyone behaved in that manner, but the majority did and we need to return to the days when the majority developed maturity. Even for non-believers saying the Lord's Prayer, and maybe we should bring it back into our schools, should be a daily reminder to develop the maturity that this country needs:

Our Father who art in Heaven, hallowed be thy name.

This acknowledges that we are really small beings that the universe, even if you don't believe God made it, is much bigger and greater than any human mind can comprehend.

They kingdom come; thy will be done.

We cannot control what happens around us, but we should quietly get on with doing what we can.

Give us this day our daily bread.

This should remind us not to be greedy, that everyone having what we need for the day is enough.

And forgive us our trespasses as we forgive those who trespass against us.

Everyone makes mistakes, even do wrong things but when we remember that we are not perfect either, we should be more willing to forgive.

Lead us not into temptation but deliver us from evil.

Bad behaviour in others should create better behaviour in us.

For thine is the glory for ever and ever.

When we leave this world, it's not what we have but how we behaved that will be remembered.

Yes, let's grow up Australia, remind ourselves each day that we only pass through this world once and what we do will definitely out-last what we have, even what we say.

When Are We Going to God?

I was in the Supermarket, having spoken to an elderly member of our congregation about how bad our world was, and the question was asked if we would make it to Christmas which was just a few weeks away. As I was making my way to the checkout, a little voice that belonged to a child in one of my Scripture classes, asked me "When are we going to God?"

The puzzled look on my face made her realise that the question hadn't come out correctly and she continued until it became clear that what she really was asking was when would we be having the next Scripture lesson, which I was able to tell her would be the next day, after which she ran off happily to catch up with her mother.

But the initial question still hung in the air.

The first thought that I jumped to, given the previous conversation, was when will we be going to be with God in Heaven? The answer to that is, no one knows. For that to happen, we either have to die, and no one knows when that will be, or Jesus has to return, and no one knows when that is going to happen either. Matthew 24:36 tells us: "But of that day and hour knoweth no *man*, no, not the angels of heaven, but my Father only."

Later, however, I thought about all the other times that we can or have to go to God.

We have to go to God, to have our sins forgiven, there is no other way for us to get to Heaven. "Jesus saith unto him, I am the way, the truth, and the life: no man cometh unto the Father, but by me." (John 14:6)

Then each day we go to God, with our prayers and petitions, our heartaches, and joys and the best thing is that we don't have to go to a scripture class, church, or anywhere special, we can go to God just where we are, no matter where that is.

So, in answer to the question, the answer is a simple – ANYTIME.

While We Wait

We desperately needed rain for our thirsty paddocks. Memories of the last drought were still foremost in our minds. We knew that there was nothing we could do to make it rain, only God could do that, and He would when the time was right. It didn't matter what the forecasters said, God controls the weather, not us, not them.

I was aware that many people pray to God for things that they cannot make happen themselves. Maybe it's for a family member to ask Jesus into their lives, for someone to stop some addictive habit, or just something that seems to be out of their reach. These are hard times for anyone regardless of what the request is.

We are not the only people who have had to wait a long time for God to answer their prayers. Hannah comes to mind. The people of Israel had to wait many times for God to answer their prayers.

It's hard to know what we can do while we are waiting for God to answer our prayers. So, I went looking.

Micah 7:7 says: "Therefore I will look unto the LORD; I will wait for the God of my salvation: my God will hear me." When it feels as if our prayers have not been listened to, this verse tells us that yes, God has heard them but waiting doesn't mean that we have to sit down and do nothing.

Psalm 130:5 tells us what David did "I wait for the LORD, my soul doth wait, and in his word do I hope." and we can do the same because the God he trusted is the same God we trust today.

So, let's just get on with the things that need to be done, the everyday things and that way we will be ready when God answers after all it will be hard to appreciate God's answers to their fullest if we have a lot of ordinary jobs to catch up on when He answers. Proverbs 3:5 "Trust in the LORD with all thine heart; and lean not unto thine own understanding."

Wisdom

Are you searching for wisdom in our current world?

"Be very careful, then, how you live—not as unwise but as wise, making the most of every opportunity, because the days are evil. Therefore, do not be foolish, but understand what the Lord's will is." Ephesians 5:15-17.

Many of us have been caught unprepared for the events that have happened world-wide in 2020. Some of us found that we could not secure sufficient supplies of particular products. Here in Australia, toilet paper, flour, milk, and pasta were put on restricted lists. This meant that you could only purchase one or two items at a time. For us, that wasn't a problem but for larger families it became a major issue causing stress. I know of one business that donated toilet paper to a family of five children who hadn't been able to purchase any and had been out for three days.

I'm sure that those who panic bought these products thought that they were being wise in making sure that they had sufficient supplies to get them through lock-down. They probably thought they were being like the five virgins. But by making sure that others were left in short supply, meant that it wasn't wise at all. There is that very fine line between wisdom and foolishness when it comes to being prepared.

The five wise virgins, in Matthew 25, had enough but no more than was needed, otherwise they would have had spare oil to share.

When it comes to living well during such times, we can ask God what things He can give us to do. We need to look around and find things to do that will enable us to live well. Hobbies, such as gardening, craft, cooking, and for many, writing, is just a small list of what could be used to not only help us live well but also be used by God to spread is message to the rest of the world.

What has God given you to do in any time of crisis?

Wandering in the Wilderness.

I had a phone call from a small business owner who was distressed about the rules being put forward regarding vaccine passports. If they are enforced, they would have no choice but to sell their business, as they had been advised that the current vaccines are unsuitable for them due to health issues.

I have similar concerns as I have health issues that make me unwilling to put myself at risk until I have greater confidence in the available products.

This is not about debating the rights or wrongs of the rules, nor is it about the mark of the beast, even though I'm sure this is a foretaste of what that situation might be like for those who have to actually live through it. It's not even about our rights as Australians.

My concerns are more about the practical issues, such as shopping if the rules come into being. A number of people have complained about not being able to purchase much needed items during lockdown. For those of us who abstain from being vaccinated it means that we will, effectively, be placed in permanent lockdown. I must confess to responding to this by debating the pros and cons of stockpiling goods. The debate won on the futilely of such a strategy as even I cannot foresee my future needs and desires.

As I prayed with this person, through tears, we acknowledged that God wasn't surprised by this situation, that He had an answer already available. We even acknowledged that He often waits until 11:59:59 to give us that answer.

In the following days, I was reminded that God had helped people in this situation before. Deuteronomy 29:5 says, "I have led you forty years in the wilderness: your clothes have not grown old on you, and your shoes have not grown old on your feet." If God could provide for up to two million people for forty years, with children constantly being added to the number and growing, then surely, He can do the same for us. What He has done before, He is capable of doing again.

Prayer:

Lord, only you know what our future holds, forgive us for not trusting you enough to wait for your answer to be delivered. We also pray for those who are working to make sure that our rights are protected, bless them with courage, tenacity, wisdom, and endurance to see this matter through to the bitter end. Amen

Other Books by this Author
All these books, with the exception of *Whispers from on High*, are available as eBooks.

Turning Water into Wine
100 Stories of God's Hand in Life

More Water into Wine
100 Stories of God's Hand in Life

Still More Water into Wine
100 Stories of God's Hand in Life

Reflections
Australian Stories from my Father's Past

365 Glasses of Wine
Short Devotionals for each day of the year

Conversations with Myself – Volume 1
100 Stories of Hope, Faith, and Determination

Whispers from on High
Poems and short stories

Fireside Stories – With Wendy Brown
Australian Family Tales

Christmas Journeys – A Trilogy
3 Stories of Love and Family, spanning across the decades.

You're: Healing Broken Hearts in Huntersville
A collection of short stories featuring the broken hearted, and God's healing presence, in the small town of Huntersville

Like Father, Like Son.
A novel about family, loyalty, and corporate espionage.

Follow Helen Brown on:
Facebook: https://www.facebook.com/HelenBrownCollection/

Instagram: https://www.instagram.com/helen_brown_books/

Pinterest: https://www.pinterest.com.au/helenbrown58726/

Connect with Reading Stones for other great reads:
https://www.facebook.com/Reading-Stones-Publishing-and-Editing-Services-252366958298920

www.ingramcontent.com/pod-product-compliance
Lightning Source LLC
Chambersburg PA
CBHW020138130526
44591CB00030B/117